12106093

Conceptual Overview

Mostly Magnets was written to provide hands-on activities involving magnetism for students in grades two through eight. Magnetism has always held a fascination for young people, probably because it seems almost magical in its unseen effects. Since magnetism has so many everyday applications in modern life, students need to learn about it as a legitimate area of physical science, rather than a novelty.

An important theme of this book is *magnetic interaction* which takes place either between the magnetic fields of two magnets or between a magnet and a material such as soft iron in which a magnetic field can be induced. In this book, popular terms like *attract, repel,* and *stick to* are used in an effort to increase students' understanding of terms they already know and use. It is imperative that the term *magnetic interaction* be added to students' vocabulary.

The following is a list of the concepts which the investigations in this book apply:

- Natural magnets are found in some rocks which contain iron. Magnets can also be made from iron, steel, nickel, cobalt, rare earths, and the alloys of these metals.

- Every magnet has a magnetic field which interacts with the magnetic fields of objects containing iron or other magnetic materials. Most magnetic objects students will use and be acquainted with are made of some form of iron.

- Magnets usually have two poles, a north-seeking and a south-seeking.

- The magnetic power of a magnet is strongest near its poles and weakest midway between them.

- When two magnets are placed near one another, they react according to the poles that are near one another. Unlike poles attract, and like poles repel.

- When quantified, the magnetic powers of attraction and repulsion are mathematically equal.

- Magnets can attract magnetic materials through all nonmagnetic and most magnetic materials.

- Magnetic materials, including iron bits, can be found in sand and other types of soil.

- Magnetic fields vary in strength.

- Iron bits can be sprinkled on paper on a magnet to reveal the magnetic field lines. When this is done with a map of the globe, it illustrates that the earth has a magnetic field.

- Two magnets together have a single magnetic field and should be considered one magnet. One 2-unit magnet has a stronger magnetic field than one of its units but less than the combined strength of the two units tested separately.

- It is possible to magnetize an iron or steel object by stroking it with a magnet.

- Tapping a magnet in a strong magnetic field will increase its strength, while tapping it in a weak magnetic field will decrease its strength.

- A directional compass can be constructed using a magnetized sewing needle.

- Since magnetic force is greater than that of gravity, magnetism can be used to defy gravity in various ways.

- An electromagnet can be constructed using a battery, insulated wire, and a nail.

- It is possible to measure magnetic force (attraction and repulsion) in newtons using a spring scale.

Systems and Interactions and *Energy* are themes that permeate all of the investigations of this book. Numerous activities also apply concepts of *Scale* and *Structure*. Since many of the concepts in this book might be difficult for young students to understand, some simplifications have been made. The intent has been to produce a book of both scientific and educational value, a goal with which we trust our physicist friends will sympathize. The editors welcome any constructive comments sequencing of lessons, materials recommended, or any other rel

D1211170

What I Know About Magnets

1. What can a magnet do?

2. How many poles does a magnet have?

3. Could you make a magnet yourself?

4. What would happen if you put a crayon near a magnet?

5. What part of a magnet has the most magnetic strength?

6. What would happen if you put two magnets together?

7. Where could you get magnetic materials outdoors?

8. Where does the needle on a magnetic compass point?

9. What would happen if you put a paper clip near a magnet?

10. Could you make a compass yourself?

11. What would happen if you hit or drop a magnet?

12. Which is stronger, magnetism or gravity?

[This student inventory is intended as a pretest and/or posttest. The questions may also be used as the basis for a class discussion.]

AIMS (Activities Integrating Mathematics and Science) began in 1981 with a grant from the National Science Foundation. The non-profit AIMS Education Foundation publishes hands-on instructional materials (books and the monthly AIMS Newsletter) that integrate curricular disciplines such as mathematics, science, language arts, and social studies. The Foundation sponsors a national program of professional development through which educators may gain both an understanding of the AIMS philosophy and expertise in teaching by integrated, hands-on methods.

ISBN 1-881431-29-0

Printed in the United States of America

Mostly Magnets

EDITOR

GRETCHEN WINKLEMAN
Editor
AIMS Education Foundation

AUTHORS

EVALYN HOOVER
Science Specialist
Fresno Unified School District

MAUREEN MURPHY ALLEN
Science Resource Specialist
Irvine Unified School District

SHERYL MERCIER
Science/Health Coordinator
Fresno Unified School District

DEBBY DEAL
Science Resource Specialist
Irvine Unified School District

HOWARD LARIMER
Science Specialist
Fresno Unified School District

GALE PHILIPS KAHN
Science Resource Specialist
Irvine Unified School District

VINCENT SIPKOVICH
Science Resource Specialist
Irvine Unified School District

ILLUSTRATORS

Brenda Howsepian   Sheryl Mercier   Max Cantu   Lori Hammeras

Mostly Magnets has been developed through a cooperative program
involving the Fresno Unified School District, Irvine Unified School District,
and the AIMS Education Foundation.

TABLE OF CONTENTS

RESOURCE SECTION

Math content

	Using number sense & numeration	Using Venn diagram & set theory	Using whole number operations	Measuring length	Measuring mass	Measuring force	Using geometry & spatial sense	Identifying & using inequalities	Averaging	Using percent, fractions, decimals	Graphing
Stick to It		✔									
What Will a Magnet Attract?	✔										✔
A Sorting Challenge		✔									
Fish and Clips			✔		✔			✔	✔		✔
Holding Power	✔		✔		✔			✔			✔
Will a Magnet Attract Through These?											
Through It All	✔		✔								
How Close Can You Get?	✔			✔							
Mining with Magnets			✔		✔			✔			
Magnetic Lines							✔				
Face to Face											
Hungry Hounds											
Floating Magnets				✔							
Defying Gravity											
Magnetic Tug of War			✔	✔					✔		
Making Magnets	✔	✔									✔
Make a Compass							✔				
Make an Electromagnet	✔			✔			✔				
What's the Attraction?						✔			✔	✔	✔
Magnets Apart						✔			✔	✔	✔

Science Processing Skills

	Observing	Making & testing hypotheses	Classifying & sorting	Collecting & organizing data	Identifying & controling variables	Reporting data	Interpreting data
Stick to It	✓		✓	✓		✓	✓
What Will a Magnet Attract?		✓	✓	✓		✓	✓
A Sorting Challenge		✓	✓			✓	
Fish and Clips				✓		✓	✓
Holding Power	✓	✓		✓	✓	✓	✓
Will a Magnet Attract Through These?	✓	✓	✓			✓	
Through It All	✓	✓			✓	✓	✓
How Close Can You Get?	✓	✓				✓	✓
Mining with Magnets	✓	✓	✓		✓	✓	✓
Magnetic Lines	✓	✓		✓		✓	✓
Face to Face	✓	✓			✓	✓	✓
Hungry Hounds	✓	✓			✓		✓
Floating Magnets	✓	✓			✓	✓	✓
Defying Gravity	✓	✓			✓	✓	✓
Magnetic Tug of War	✓	✓			✓	✓	✓
Making Magnets	✓	✓		✓	✓	✓	✓
Make a Compass	✓				✓	✓	✓
Make an Electromagnet	✓	✓			✓		✓
What's the Attraction?	✓	✓		✓		✓	✓
Magnets Apart	✓	✓		✓		✓	✓

I HEAR, AND I FORGET
I SEE, AND I REMEMBER
I DO, AND I UNDERSTAND

-Chinese Proverb

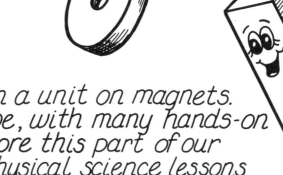

Dear Parents,

Soon our class will begin a unit on magnets. Sound like fun? It will be, with many hands-on activities to help us explore this part of our wonderful world. These physical science lessons combine math with science processing skills. We hope that this unit helps students to learn, but we also hope it increases their enthusiasm for learning in math, science, and other areas. We trust you see some of this enthusiasm at home.

We will be warning students to use magnets carefully. Remember that placing magnets near computer discs, television sets, wind-up watches, or credit cards may cause damage.

Our activities require a variety of magnets. If you have any unused magnets, we would be happy to have them to use in this unit. Do not send any of great value, but if you want to help, label the magnets with your student's name and send them along.

Thank you,

_____

Teacher

Stick To It

I. Science Topic Area   Physical science: magnetism, magnet interaction

    Math Topic Area   Venn diagram

II. Introductory Statement

Students will classify objects in the classroom according to whether or not they interact with magnets.

III. Math Content

Numeration
Venn diagram

Science Processing Skills

Observing
Classifying & sorting
Collecting & organizing data
Reporting data
Interpreting data

IV. Materials

Supply of *sticky notes* in 2 colors (or 1 color marked *yes & no*)
Large newsprint with charts from activity sheets *To What Will a Magnet Stick?* and *In or Out of the Circle*
Caution signs
Magnets (1 per student)

V. Key Question

What kinds of objects in our classroom will stick to a magnet?

VI. Background Information

Magnetism is usually defined and taught by focussing on the individual magnet and its magnetic field. It is important to realize that *for magnetic force to be observed, there must be an interaction, either between the magnetic fields of magnets or between a magnet and a material such as soft iron in which a magnetic field can be induced.* In other words, a magnet does not ever just lie somewhere; even when no one is using it to attract or repel things, its magnetic field is always busy interacting with other magnetic fields.

In this book, a conscious effort has been made to use familiar vocabulary. As a result, magnets are referred to in this book as *attracting* or *repelling* materials, and objects are said to *stick to* magnets. These are not contradictions of the

magnetic interaction concept, but attempts to begin with terms that most students already use. Needless to say, it is expected that students will increase their understanding of magnetism and correct their misconceptions about it as they participate in the various investigations. In addition, it is imperative that students learn to use and understand the term *magnetic interaction* as soon as possible. For a fuller explanation of this and other topics related to magnetism, please read *Science Information* beginning on page 92.

The *Venn diagram* is a way of visualizing sets of objects or materials. To use a Venn diagram, you must have three things: a set of something with distinguishable characteristics, a property that each set member either has or lacks, and some way of deciding whether or not each member has the identified property.

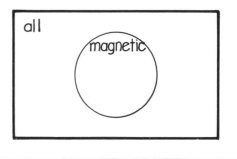

VII. Management

1. Mark sticky notes *yes* and *no* or *magnetic* and *nonmagnetic*, depending on age and reading ability of students.
2. Beforehand, make copies of the large and small caution signs to use in the classroom and to send home.
3. Be sure to allow ample time for the exploratory part of this lesson; it is an essential introductory learning experience.

VIII. Procedure

1. Demonstrate magnetism by hiding a magnet in your pocket, then casually bringing your

scissors to the outside of the pocket. Remove your hand and let the scissors remain stuck to your clothing. How many students noticed?

2. Place two magnets on the overhead projector. Turn the projector on, and let the students guess what they are. Place the magnets so that they repel each other. Bring one toward the other, and let students see the second one *scoot* away. Then turn the magnets so that they attract. When one jumps toward the other, the class will probably identify the objects as magnets.

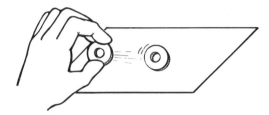

3. Discuss briefly how magnets are used in everyday life. Include ways we can guard against damaging property with our magnets.
4. Post caution signs on computers and other appliances. Set aside any wind-up watches.
5. Ask the *Key Question*: "What kinds of objects in our classroom will stick to a magnet?"
6. Distribute magnets, so that students can test items from their desks, to see if the magnets will stick to them.
7. As students continue to test items from their desks and around the room, encourage them to use the *sticky notes* on objects to which their magnets do or do not stick. (Plan to leave some items labeled for a few days to remind students about magnetism in their environment.)
8. Place the large chart *To What Will a Magnet Stick?* on the floor. Have students place items in the appropriate spaces.
9. Use activity sheets to record data by listing or drawing pictures. Discuss with the students that objects *stick to* or *are attracted to* a magnet because they are made of a material (usually iron) which is magnetic.
10. Place the large chart *In or Out of the Circle?* on the floor.
11. Place some items not yet tested inside the rectangle but outside the circle.
12. Encourage students to predict whether or not the magnet is going to stick to each object. Then test it. If it sticks to the magnet, place it in the circle; if not, put it back in the rectangle outside the circle.
13. Have students list or draw objects in the appropriate spaces to record their observations.

IX. Discussion
1. To what objects did the magnets stick? How are these objects alike?
2. Do magnets attract all objects made of metal?
3. Can a magnet pick up everything it attracts? How do you know?

4. What do we mean when we say a magnet sticks to something? What could we say instead?
5. How can you predict whether or not a magnet will attract a certain object?
6. When you hold a magnet near a magnetic object, what happens to the magnet? What happens to the object?

X. Extensions
Repeat steps 10-13 with a Venn diagram of a different shape, as shown.

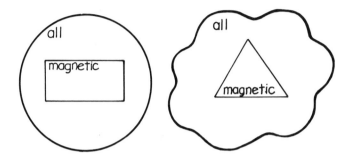

XI. Curriculum Correlations
Reading: Have students look in the school library for information on William Gilbert and other scientists who have done research on magnets.
Creative writing: Have students write stories about using a magnet to play a trick on a friend.

XII. Home Link
Have students take the parents' letter home if they have not already done so. Include caution signs, so that when they experiment with magnets at home, they will remember to be careful.

To what will a magnet stick?

My magnet sticks to:	My magnet does not stick to:

3

Name _____

In or Out of the Circle?

all

magnetic

CAUTION

Magnets should not be held near these things:

TV
VCR
microwave oven
computer
radio
loudspeakers
credit cards

wind up watches
computer discs
cassette tapes
tape recorders
telephones
answering machines
video tapes

5

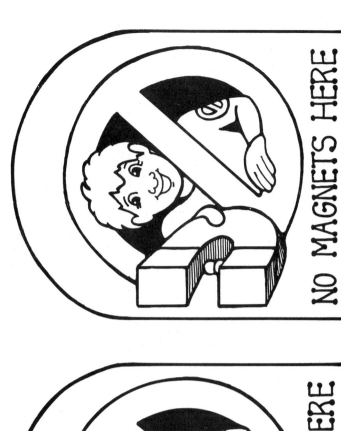 NO MAGNETS HERE

 NO MAGNETS HERE

 NO MAGNETS HERE

 NO MAGNETS HERE

 NO MAGNETS HERE

 NO MAGNETS HERE

What Will a Magnet Attract?

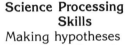

I. Science Topic Area

Physical science:
  magnetism,
  magnetic interaction

Math Topic Area

Graphing

II. Introductory Statement

The students will predict and then test objects for their magnetic interaction.

III. Math Content

Numeration
Graphing

Science Processing Skills

Making hypotheses
Classifying & sorting
Collecting &
  organizing data
Reporting data

IV. Materials

Magnets
Scissors
Paste
Collections of objects (see activity sheets)

V. Key Question

What will a magnet attract?

VI. Background Information

All substances actually display magnetic properties, but most show them to such a very small degree that we usually consider these materials nonmagnetic. Highly sophisticated scientific equipment is needed to detect magnetic characteristics at these low levels. On the other hand, a few metallic elements such as iron, nickel, cobalt, rare earths, plus some of their alloys like steel and strontium ferrite display magnetic properties strongly enough to be considered *magnetic,* or—more properly—*ferromagnetic* (the *ferro*– means iron). All metals are not considered magnetic, a common misconception easily corrected by observing a common magnet's effect on brass, copper, or aluminum. See *Science Information* beginning on page 92 for additional information.

VII. Management

1. If students have not had experience with magnets, use the AIMS investigation *Stick to it* or allow time for free exploration before using this lesson.
2. Most paper fasteners are brass and therefore nonmagnetic, but some newer ones have a magnetic coating. It is useful to use metallic but nonmagnetic items to promote appropriate generalizations.
3. Three levels of activity sheets have been included. *Level 1* is intended as a structured activity for primaries, *Level 2* as a less structured activity for either primaries or intermediates, and *Level 3* as a *Home Link,* structured activity for families to enjoy together.

VIII. Procedure

Activity 1

1. This lesson is best used as a whole class activity.
2. Have students handle the objects pictured on the activity sheet *Mighty Magnet,* discussing whether or not they think various objects are magnetic.
3. Ask the *Key Question:* "What will a magnet attract?"
4. Have students cut out the small pictures on the activity sheet.

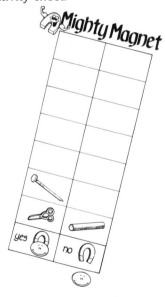

5. Discuss *predicting* on a level your students can understand. It is really *telling ahead of time*; the concept of *guessing* may also be used, as long as students understand that they should use information they already have to make guesses reasonable.
6. Students predict whether or not the magnet will attract each object pictured by placing its

picture in a box over the *yes* or *no*. (Be sure to build from the bottom up as a regular picture graph.)

7. Distribute magnets. Students test each item to see whether or not their predictions were correct and reposition pictures as necessary.
8. Discuss the testing, especially objects that seem to have caused any confusion. Let students retest if necessary.
9. Paste pictures in place.
10. Discuss the finished picture graphs together.

Activity 2
1. On the activity sheet *What Will a Magnet Attract? (Part 1)*, suggest that each group predict which objects will be attracted by the magnet.
2. Test each one and record results by coloring *yes* or *no*.
3. Discuss as a class how well groups' predictions match their test results. Try to find reasons for discrepancies.
4. On the activity sheet *What will a Magnet Attract? (Part 2)*, have students list or draw pictures of all objects they want to test.
5. Have students predict which of these will be attracted magnetically. Encourage students to make their own individual predictions this time, instead of having the groups decide.
6. Test each object with a magnet and record results.
7. As a class, discuss what happened. Have students write a sentence to share what they learned.

Activity 3
Recommended for use as a *Home Link*
1. At school, discuss the three types of magnets pictured at the left, so that students will understand they can use any shape or size of magnet to do the investigation at home.
2. Discuss the directions and make predictions.
3. Finish the investigation at home.

IX. Discussion
1. What do you know about magnets that should help you make good predictions?
2. What is the most important piece of information about an object that will help you make a good prediction about its magnetic attraction? (whether it is made of iron or some other magnetic material)
3. How many objects were attracted to the magnet? . . . not attracted?
4. Were you surprised by the reaction of any of the objects? Why? What happened?
5. Did everyone have the same results? What caused the differences? (You may need to retest to find out.)

X. Extension
Discuss whether more objects in the world are magnetic or nonmagnetic. How would you find out?

XI. Curriculum Correlations
Creative writing: List together and discuss words describing the action of a magnet or an object attracted: pull, draw, move, stick, etc. Write poems about magnets, using these words.
Social studies: Visit a place where industrial electromagnets are used. Possibilities could include local factories, a scrap metal (or recycling) company, or an automobile demolition concern.

XII. Home Link
See *Activity 3*, above.

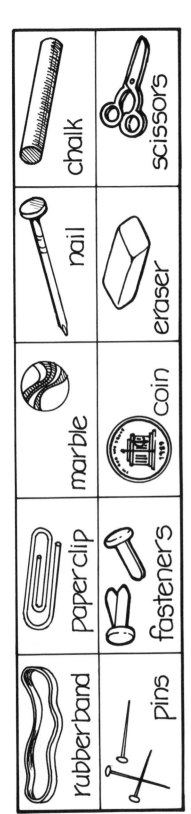

Name _____

Mighty Magnet

yes	no

Predict, place pictures in the yes or no side. Test objects with a magnet. Glue down pictures in the correct column.

What Will a Magnet Attract?

(Level 1)

If you think the magnet will attract an object, draw a ring around the picture.

Test with a magnet.

Did the magnet attract it? Color [yes] or [no]

		Results				Results
	ping pong ball	yes	no		key	yes | no
	nail	yes	no		screw	yes | no
	chalk	yes	no		dime	yes | no
	wire	yes	no		battery	yes | no
	rubber band	yes	no		juice can	yes | no
	wooden pencil	yes	no		magnet	yes | no
	twist tie	yes	no		penny	yes | no
	soft drink can	yes	no		paper clip	yes | no

Write a sentence about what you learned.

_____

10

What Will A Magnet Attract?

(Level 2)

Magnetic attraction is a force that makes some things move toward a magnet.

Choose some things to test with your magnet.

Use an **X** to mark the objects that you think will be attracted.

Did the magnet attract it ? Color the |yes| or |no|.

Object	Results		Object	Results	
	yes	no		yes	no
	yes	no		yes	no
	yes	no		yes	no
	yes	no		yes	no
	yes	no		yes	no
	yes	no		yes	no
	yes	no		yes	no
	yes	no		yes	no

Write a sentence about what you learned.

What Will a Magnet Attract?

Magnetic attraction is a force that makes some things move toward a magnet.

Of the objects listed below, which will a magnet attract?

Make your prediction. Record your results.

Prediction	**Object**	**Results** yes	no
	thumbtacks		
	nail		
	toothpicks		
	penny		
	pin		
	sand		
	pen		
	bits of paper		
	paper clips		
	tin foil		
	dime		
	steel wool		
	leather		
	glass		
	tin can		
	cloth		
	scissors		
	brass paper fastener		
	rubber bands		
	needle		
	plastic		
	magnet		

horseshoe

ring

bar

Conclusion: _____

_____

_____

How Are Magnets Made?

There are three different kinds of magnets: natural, temporary, and permanent. Each kind is made in a different way.

Natural magnets are rocks with a lot of iron in them. Magnetite is an example of rock that is naturally magnetic. Natural magnets are magnetic when they are found in the ground. No one has to do anything to them, because they are already magnets.

Temporary magnets are called that because they are weak and last only a short time. They are made from pure ("soft") iron. One way to make a temporary magnet is to stroke a soft iron object (like a nail) with a magnet.

temporary magnet

electromagnet

Another way is to use an electromagnet, which is a coil of wire through which electric current can be passed. The iron is put inside the coil. When the electricity is turned on, a strong electric

charge is sent through the wire. This creates a strong magnetic field and turns the iron into a magnet. This kind of magnet is called temporary because the magnet loses most of its magnetic power when the electricity is turned off.

Permanent magnets are made from "hard" iron, which is iron plus some other special materials. Steel is a hard iron, so it makes good permanent magnets. If we stroke steel scissors they will be magnetized. These are called permanent magnets because they are strong and because they hold their magnetism for a long time.

A ceramic magnet is a special kind of permanent magnet. The ring magnets we use in school are ceramic magnets. They are made from a form of iron called strontium ferrite.

This powder is pressed into molds. Then it is put into a very hot oven where it is heated to 2250 degrees Fahrenheit. As these future magnets cool, they shrink slightly. Then they are magnetized in an electromagnet to align the domains. The flat sides of ring magnets become their poles.

A Sorting Challenge

I. Science Topic Area   Physical science:
                                magnetism,
                                magnetic sorting

Math Topic Area   Venn diagram

II. Introductory Statement
The students will sort small objects manually and then will experience the increased efficiency of sorting them magnetically.

III. Math Content   **Science Processing Skills**

Venn Diagram   Making hypotheses
                Classifying & sorting
                Reporting data

IV. Materials
For the class: Clock with second hand
For each group:
  Magnets
  Plastic bag with mixture of paper clips and brass (nonmagnetic) paper fasteners
  Bag with mixture of salt and iron filings or bits
  Tweezers

V. Key Question
How can we sort into magnetic and nonmagnetic sets?

VI. Background Information
In industry, magnets are often utilized to sort magnetic materials from nonmagnetic because of the increased efficiency. The main purpose of this lesson is to introduce students to such applications. A secondary benefit, however, can be to help them learn experientially that all metals are not magnetic, a common misconception. For further information, see *Science Information* beginning on page 92.

See the explanation of the *Venn diagram* in *Stick to It* on page 1.

VII. Management
1. Students should work in groups of 2 - 5.
2. For directions on obtaining iron bits from sand or dirt, see *Mining with Magnets*, beginning on page 45.
3. In *Part 1*, emphasize the difference in time between sorting manually and by magnet; avoid competition between groups.
4. *Part 2* has exciting opportunities for creative problem-solving. Allow time for students to brainstorm ways of sorting; try a few as time allows.
5. In *Part 2*, you may wish to cover each magnet with *one* layer of plastic wrap or put the magnet in a *thin* plastic bag. Ring magnets are difficult, because the iron bits get into the holes.
6. In the removal of iron bits from magnets in *Part 2*, remind students that in industry, electromagnets would be used, and when the power is turned off, the iron bits (or other magnetic materials) would fall from the electromagnet.

VIII. Procedure
Part 1
1. Ask the *Key Question:* "How can we sort into magnetic and nonmagnetic sets?" (manually or by using magnets) Have them predict which method would be more efficient. Guide students to realize that a way to compare the two strategies would be to time them.
2. Each pair of students should decide and note on the activity sheets which person will be the timekeeper and which the sorter.
3. Distribute bags of clips and paper fasteners.
4. Students empty their bags onto the universal set region of the Venn diagram.
5. At the signal the sorters begin sorting, placing each magnetic object (clip) in the circle and returning nonmagnetic objects to the universal set region. When sorters finish, the timekeepers of each team record the last number called.
6. Continue sorting for the second and third trials. Find the average time it took.
7. Distribute magnets and discuss how the class thinks results might differ when they use magnets.
8. Time the activity in the same way.
9. Discuss and record what was learned.

Part 2
(Reuse the *Venn diagram* sorting sheet, but not the timed report.)

1. Distribute bags of salt and iron bits. Discuss possible contents of the bags. Tell students what is in the bags.
2. Repeat the *Key Question:* "How can we sort into magnetic and nonmagnetic sets?" Present tweezers as one possible strategy; have a student try to sort manually using them!
3. Encourage students to think of other solutions, such as dissolving the salt in water. Discuss advantages and disadvantages of all solutions suggested, including the use of magnets. If at all possible, try several of the most promising strategies.
4. Carefully pour the contents of the bags onto the universal set portion of the Venn diagrams.
5. Use magnets to pick up the iron bits; remove them from the magnets and place them in the circle as the magnetic set.

IX. Discussion
1. Which method of sorting was faster, manual or magnetic?
2. Why do you think the magnets helped sort faster?
3. What were some problems in the magnetic sorting? (paper fasteners being caught up with clips, removing iron bits from magnet)
4. How do you think a factory would utilize magnets in sorting? Why would they still need workers to help with such an operation?

X. Extensions
1. Think of unique ways to return the iron bits to the bags.
2. Substitute similarly sized steel and brass screws or a mixture of several types of magnetic and nonmagnetic objects in *Part 1.*
3. Using the *Part 1* activity, have a race between two groups using the two methods, but blindfold the sorters!
4. Play *Treasure Hunt.* Place paper clips, washers, screws, and nails in the bottom of a pint sized cottage cheese carton. Almost fill the carton with salt, hiding the *treasures.* Let students take turns holding a magnet over the salt and lowering it slowly. The stronger the magnet, the more fun it is to see items almost jump out of the salt.

XI. Curriculum Correlations
Language arts: List together and discuss words describing how the magnet and the other materials feel: cool, heavy, solid, round, pointed, etc. Practice using these words in sentences about magnets and other objects. Emphasize that these are adjectives or descriptors.

Reading/social studies: Use encyclopedias and other library materials to find out more about the mining of iron, especially magnetite.

Name _____

A Sorting Challenge

How can we sort into magnetic and nonmagnetic sets ?

_____

Prediction: Which method would be faster and better ?

_____

Timekeeper _____

Sorter _____

Sorting by Hand

Trial 1 _____ seconds

Trial 2 _____ seconds

Trial 3 _____ seconds

Total time _____ seconds

Average _____ seconds

Sorting by Magnet

Trial 1 _____ seconds

Trial 2 _____ seconds

Trial 3 _____ seconds

Total time _____ seconds

Average _____ seconds

We learned _____

_____

17

Name

a Sorting
Challenge

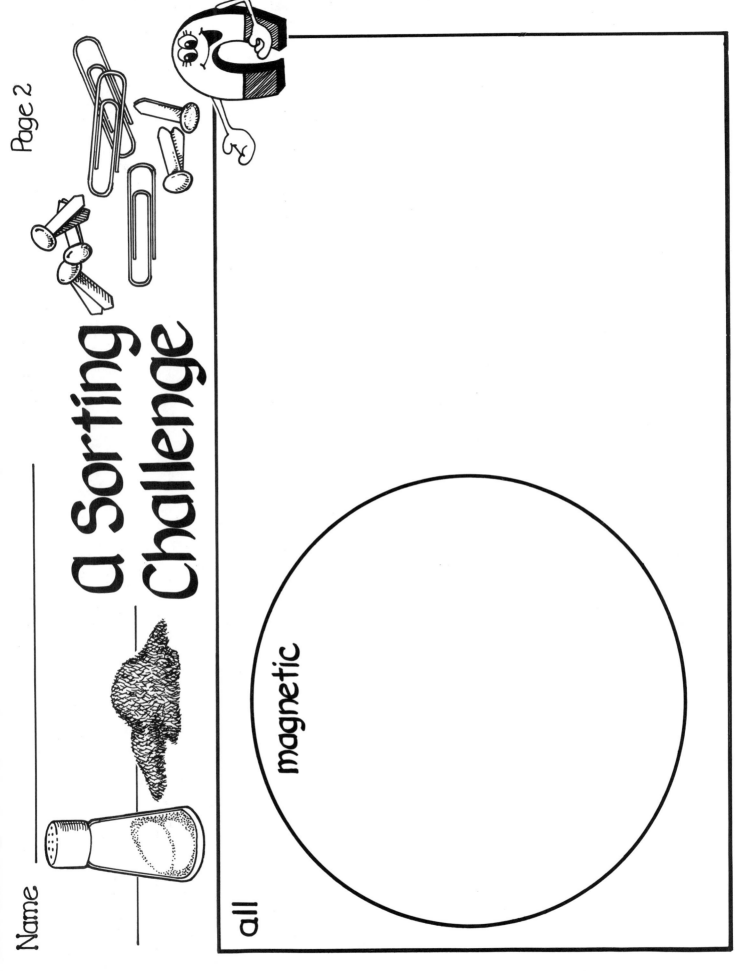

magnetic

all

18

Fish and Clips

I. Science Topic Area   Physical science: magnetism magnet strength

   Math Topic Area   Graphing

II. Introductory Statement
Students will quantify the magnet strength by measuring and averaging—by number and by mass—the small and large *fish* (paper clips) they *catch* with a magnet.

III. Math Content

Math Content	Science Processing Skills
Using whole number operations	Collecting & organizing data
Averaging	Reporting data
Measuring mass	Interpreting data
Graphing	
Inequalities	

IV. Materials
For each team:
   2 brown lunch-size bags - pools
   25 big paper clips - big fish
   35 little paper clips - little fish
   15″ string, tied to any type of magnet, attached to dowel or non-sharp pencil - fishing pole
For Part 2: balance scale with metric masses

V. Key Question
What is your average catch?

VI. Background Information
   Even if magnets are the same size and shape, they may vary in magnetic strength. Magnets also *age* (weaken) over time. This aging may be accelerated if a magnet is dropped or tapped in a weak magnetic field. See *Science Information*, beginning on page 92 for additional information.

Part 2
1. Mix big and little paper clips in one bag.
2. For Trial 1, fish for clips by dipping once.
3. Measure by number. Separate, count, record, and total the catch.
4. Measure by mass. Record both sizes of fish. Then find the combined mass.
5. Continue the other trials in the same way.
6. Briefly review the concept of *average* if necessary.
7. Find the average of the five trials, both by number and by mass.
8. Discuss your findings as a class. List the averages of all groups on the chalkboard; have students make observations about any patterns in the averages. Remember to be careful comparing the averages by number

with those by mass, because the two averages are given in different units.

VII. Management
1. Students should work in groups of 2-4 and take turns fishing within their groups.
2. Be sure all paper clips are separate from one another before fishing.
3. If your students need more experience in averaging, have them fish two or three times and average before doing the five times indicated on the activity sheet.
4. When calculating averages, express answers in whole fish with remainders dropped.

VIII. Procedure
Part 1
1. With the fishing pole, students fish for big paper clips and record the catch.
2. Fish for small clips and record the catch.
3. Build a bar graph by coloring in the appropriate blocks.
4. Discuss which catch was more, and how much more. Have students tell how they found out by using the bar graph, by subtracting, or by some other way.
5. Discuss briefly the sign for *greater than,* and fill in the blanks.
6. Conclusions may be either scientific or mathematical.

IX. Discussion
1. Did the magnet attract more small or more large clips? What two ways can you use to find out the difference between the two average catches? (bar graph or subtraction) Did any group catch the same number of small and large clips?

2. What happened when the magnet attracted the clips in the bag? Why did some clips drop off? Did this happen more with one size of clip than the other? What difference would

this make in any conclusions you draw? (The magnet didn't *attract* clips if some of them were merely hooked.)

3. Which group had the largest average catch? What made the difference?
4. What are some different ways of saying which catch was larger? (more than, greater than, less than)
5. Why did we make five trials and average them, instead of having just one trial?

X. Extensions

1. Build two class bar graphs using the averages.
2. Empty three bags of clips into one and use three magnets to fish; is the catch three times as large? Try to explain what happened.
3. Have students find some of the many ratios: small to large, small to total, large to total, etc.
4. To sort the clips for reuse, have a timed sorting race.

XI. Curriculum Correlations

Creative Writing: Have each team write an imaginary adventure story, of which the main character is a magnet. This could include leaving the factory, being purchased at a store, being given as a gift, etc.

XII. Home Link

Have students count the total number of magnets they have in their homes.

Fish and Clips

Part 1

55	
50	
45	
40	
35	
30	
25	
20	
15	
10	
5	
0	
big fish	little fish

Each clip is one fish.

Record your catches:

_____ big fish

_____ little fish

Build a bar graph with your catches:

Which is more?

How many more?

_____

Fill in the blanks with your catches.

_____ > _____

Conclusions: _____

_____

_____

_____

_____

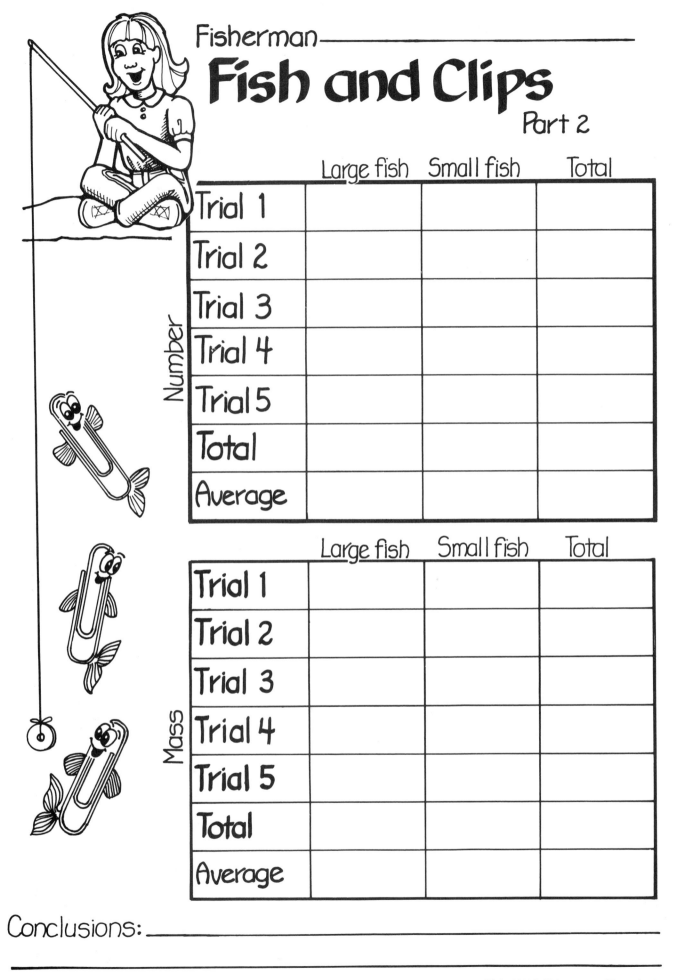

Fisherman _____

Fish and Clips
Part 2

	Large fish	Small fish	Total
Number			
Trial 1			
Trial 2			
Trial 3			
Trial 4			
Trial 5			
Total			
Average			

	Large fish	Small fish	Total
Mass			
Trial 1			
Trial 2			
Trial 3			
Trial 4			
Trial 5			
Total			
Average			

Conclusions: _____

Holding Power

I. Science Topic Area — Physical science: magnetism, magnet strength

Math Topic Area — Measuring mass, graphing

II. Introductory Statement
Students will compare the magnetic strength of two separate magnets with the magnetic strength of one 2-unit magnet; then, they will do the same with three separate magnets and one 3-unit magnet.

III. Math Content
Using number sense & numeration
Using whole number operations
Measuring mass
Identifying & using inequalities
Graphing

Science Processing Skills
Observing
Collecting & organizing data
Making & testing hypotheses
Identifying & controlling variables
Reporting data
Interpreting data

IV. Materials
For each group:
3 ceramic ring magnets (labelled with numbers if desired)
1 large paper clip, with larger end bent into a hook
70 paper clips
Balance scale and gram masses.

For the class:
Transparency or newsprint copy of *Part 2* activity sheet for class summary
Felt markers

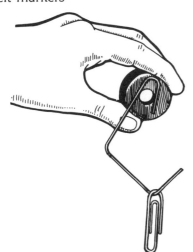

V. Key Questions
Level 1: How many paper clips will a magnet hold?
Level 2: Which would hold more paper clips, two magnets separately or two magnets together?

VI. Background Information
Magnets vary greatly in strength according to a number of factors including what materials they were made from, how they were made, how old they are, and how they have been treated. *When two (or more) magnets are placed together, they become one combined magnetic force and are considered one magnet.* Such a magnet made up of two units will be stronger than one magnet but not quite as strong as the combined strength of the two magnets tested separately. See *Science Information* beginning on page 92.

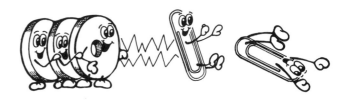

VII. Management
1. Students should work in cooperative learning groups.
2. Note that when the hook falls off, you are observing how much is too much, or how much it will *not* hold. Be sure to recheck that it will hold one less.
3. When you put two ring magnets together, they automatically have opposite poles facing one another. If you use another type of magnet, be sure they are arranged this way; it may not be obvious, especially if magnets are weak.
4. Variations in the number of clips held (even by the same magnet) may be due to a number of factors, such as the amount of magnet surface that the hook is touching, the angle at which the magnet is held, the force with which clips are placed on the hook, and whether or not some of the small clips are touching the magnet directly (they should not be). With some students, you may wish to stabilize the magnet by attaching it to a vertical magnetic surface such as a filing cabinet.

5. The vertical scale of the *Part 2* activity sheet bar graph needs to be labeled (either before duplicating or during the activity): *Clips Held - Total Quantity* or *Clips Held - Total Mass*.

6. Test several magnets beforehand so you can use the same numerical vertical scale for the whole graph. The highest total should be three separate magnets.

7. This is an excellent lesson for teaching *predicting* as a thinking skill. By having repeated opportunities to predict, students should improve their ability to use available information to predict future outcomes in a logical way. One key is to have students explain their reasons for their predictions.

VIII. Procedure

Level 1

1. Show students a magnet with hook and paper clip. Ask them the *Key Question*: "How many paper clips will a magnet hold?"

2. In groups, have students discuss and record predictions for both number and mass on activity sheets.

3. Distribute one magnet, a hook, and clips to each group. To test predictions, students hold the magnet but not the hook. Hang clips on the hook one at a time until the hook falls off.

4. Remove one clip and check the hook will hold the remaining clips.

5. Count the clips on the hook, and record test result.

6. Read together and discuss the second question on the activity sheet. Explain that when we add a second magnet, we should think of the two units or magnets together as one magnet. Guide students to note how many clips one magnet held and then to predict how many clips it will hold when the second magnet is added.

7. Repeat the testing activity using one 2-unit magnet.

Level 2 Part 1

1. Show students two separate magnets, a hook, and a paper clip. Ask them the *Key Question:* "Which will hold more paper clips, two separate magnets or one 2-unit magnet?"

2. Discuss in groups how many paper clips they think can hang on the hook with one magnet before the hook falls off. Predict also what mass the hook will hold. Record predictions on the activity sheet.

3. Distribute one magnet, a hook, and clips to each group. Test as in *Level 1*.

4. Count the clips and record this for Magnet #1. Use the balance scale to find the mass in grams, and record.

5. Set aside but do not collect Magnet #1.

6. Repeat testing with Magnet #2.

7. Find the total for the 2 magnets tested separately.

8. Repeat the testing activity using one 2-unit magnet. Explain that when we do this, we should think of the 2-unit magnet as one magnet.

Level 2 Part 2

1. Copy the test results for 2 separate magnets from *Part 1*.

2. Make and explain predictions for Magnet #3.

3. Test Magnet #3 and record results.

4. Total the 3 separate magnets.

5. Make one 3-unit magnet. Test predictions and record results.

6. Add a third magnet; predict, test, and record similarly.

7. What pattern do students begin to see? Finish the activity sheet.

Level 2 Part 3

1. Using the *Part 2* activity sheet, guide students to make individual bar graphs of their test results.

2. To make the class summary bar graph, combine data and use an appropriately numbered vertical scale (or find the class averages and use the same scale).

IX. Discussion

1. Why don't we put the paper clips right on the magnet, instead of making a hook with the big paper clip?

2. On what are you basing your prediction?

3. Why is it important to hold the magnet but not the hook?

4. Why did some students have more or fewer clips on their magnets?

5. Why might the hook hold more with a second magnet unit added?

6. Why do you think one 2-unit magnet didn't hold twice as much as a single magnet?

7. Does it matter if paper clips are hanging from one another, rather than every single one being on the hook?
8. How close were your predictions to your results? Did your predictions become more accurate with 2 and 3-unit magnets? How would you find this out?
9. Were the results surprising to you? Why?
10. What pattern do you notice in the bar graph? Is there a similar pattern in the class summary graph?

X. Extensions

1. Make a second class summary bar graph for quantity or mass, whichever you did not do during the lesson. Have students compare the two bar graphs to observe similarities. (Make scales comparable.)
2. Repeat the investigation with any magnets that had results very different from the others.
3. Put all the magnets in order by strength, according to the number or mass of clips they held.

XI. Curriculum Correlations

Drama: Have students dramatize the investigation in pantomime. Have a student stand on a chair to represent the magnet, a second student the hook, and others as the paper clips.

Social studies/language arts/art: Make a booklet showing the different uses for magnets, such as industrial, scientific, compass, kitchen-type, toys, loudspeakers, etc.

Holding Power

Names _____

_____

_____

_____

Level 1

How many paper clips will a magnet hold ?

	My guess	Test result

How many paper clips will ⬤ hold ?

	My guess	Test result

Were you surprised ? _____

Why ? _____

Holding Power

Names _____

_____

_____

_____

Level 2 Part 1

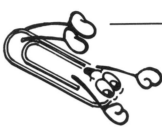

Which will hold more paper clips, two separate magnets or one 2-unit magnet?

	Prediction		Test Result	
	Number of paper clips	Mass	Number of paper clips	Mass
Magnet #1		g		g
Magnet #2		g		g
Total of 2 separate magnets		g		g
One 2-unit magnet		g		g

What did you find out? _____

_____

Holding Power

Level 2 Part 2

Find the total of 3 magnets tested separately.

	Prediction		Test Results	
	Number of Paper Clips	Mass	Number of Paper Clips	Mass
Total of 2 separate magnets		g		g
Magnet #3		g		g
Total of 3 separate magnets		g		g

What do you think will happen if you use one 3-unit magnet?

_____

_____

	Prediction		Test Results	
	Number of Paper Clips	Mass	Number of Paper Clips	Mass
One 3-unit magnet		g		g

Which held more paper clips, 3 separate magnets or one 3-unit magnet? Explain. _____

_____

Holding Power

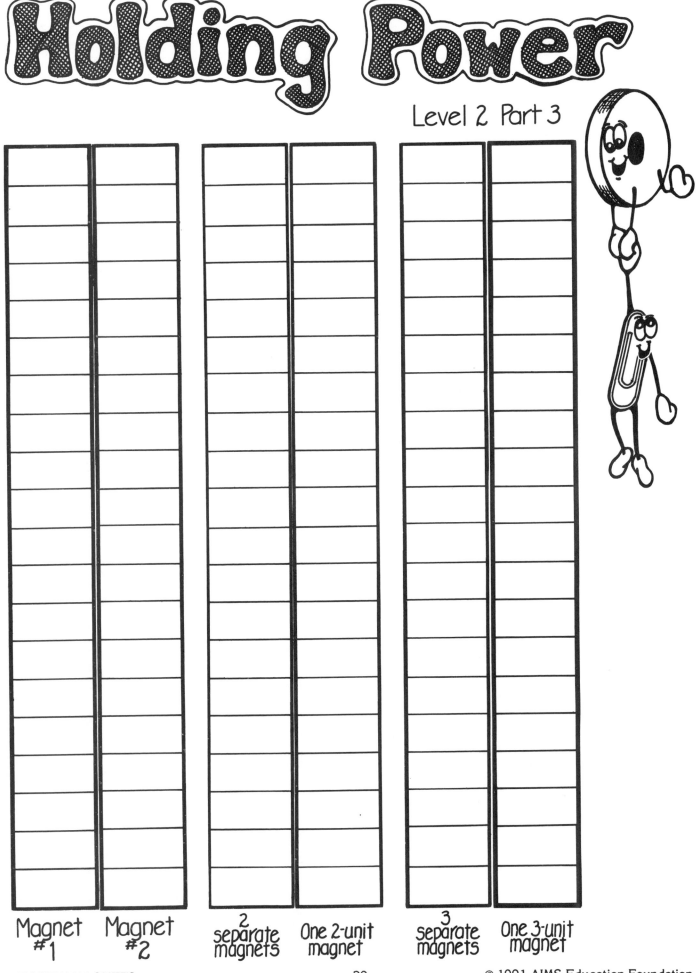

Magnet #1	Magnet #2	2 separate magnets	One 2-unit magnet	3 separate magnets	One 3-unit magnet

WHAT MAKES A THING MAGNETIC?

Many magnets are made of steel, which is iron plus some other things. Iron and steel are made up of many magnetic domains. Each domain is a very small area with billions of atoms. In an ordinary scissor blade, these domains face in different directions.

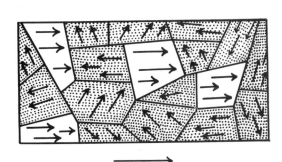

North pole of a magnet

We would say:

The domains are unaligned.
The scissor blade does not have a magnetic field
It will not attract magnetic objects.

One way to change the steel into a magnet is to stroke the scissor blade with a magnet. When you do this, the domains change and the scissor blade starts to develop a magnetic field of its own. In the drawing above, find a domain that already faces north. Now look below. What happened to that domain? Now look at another domain that faces some other

direction. How did it change? This is what happens
inside the scissor blade when it becomes slightly
magnetized.

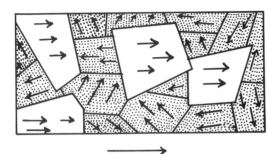

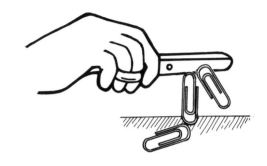

North pole of a magnet

We would say:

The domains are partly aligned.
The scissor blade has a weak magnetic field.
The scissor blade is a weak magnet.
It will pick up iron bits and other objects of small mass.

As these north-facing domains grow larger, the scissor
blade becomes a still stronger magnet.

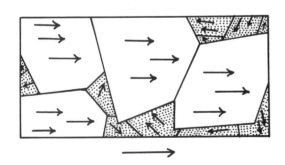

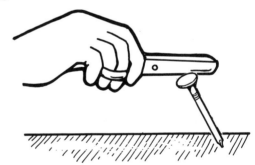

North pole of a magnet

We would say:

The domains are mostly aligned.
The scissor blade has a strong magnetic field.
The scissor blade is a strong magnet.
It will pick up more massive objects.

Will a Magnet Attract Through These?

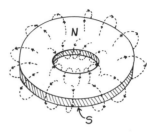

I. Science Topic Area:
Physical science: magnetism, magnetic interaction through materials

II. Introductory Statement
Students will investigate the capacity and limitations of a magnet to attract a magnetic object (paper clip) through a variety of magnetic and nonmagnetic materials.

III. Science Processing Skills
Observing
Making & testing hypotheses
Reporting data
Classifying & sorting

IV. Materials
For each group:
Magnets
Paper clips
Wooden ruler
15cm square corrugated cardboard
Fabric
Tin foil
Clear plastic cup with 3-5 cm of water
Tin can (empty, tuna-size, no lid, edges taped)
Shoe
Plastic pattern block
Glass jar, without lid

V. Key Question
Through which materials will a magnet and a paper clip interact?

VI. Background Information
A *magnetic field* is the space around a magnet in which there is a concentration of magnetic force. Magnetic fields are strongest near the north-seeking and south-seeking poles. The shape of a magnet's magnetic field is shown by the *magnetic field lines* that spread out from both poles and meet in a series of extended arcs.

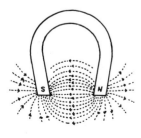
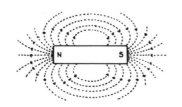

Magnetic fields are able to pass through nonmagnetic materials. This can be demonstrated by placing a piece of paper between a magnet and a small magnetic object such as a paper clip; the magnetic interaction through the paper should be readily observable. If, however, the distance between the magnet and the clip is increased, the interaction may become too weak to be observed, even though the magnetic fields are still present. The effect of such nonmagnetic materials on the magnetic interaction is negligible; the main factor is the distance involved.

The effect of magnetic materials on the situation is different. If the magnet and the clip (or two magnets) are placed on a table on opposite sides of a *tin* (steel) can and outside it, the magnetic fields will go around the can. If, on the other hand, the magnet and the clip are put inside and outside the bottom of the can, there will be magnetic interaction between them through the magnetic material. There will also be some induced magnetism by which the can takes on some magnetism; however, the clip should move when the magnet is moved, showing that the interaction is between the magnet and the clip. If however, the magnet is too weak, the magnetic object too massive, or the distance between them too great, the effects of the magnetic interaction may not be observable even though the magnetic fields are still present. See *Science Information*, beginning on page 92 for more information.

VII. Management
1. Students should work in cooperative learning groups.
2. Each student will test every item. Some, such as the ruler and the foil, they can place over a clip on the table and then try to pick it up. Part of the fun can be deciding how to do the testing. Here are some ideas for handling the more awkward materials:
   - Water: Drop the clip into the water, and hold the magnet at the surface of the water.

- Tin can, glass jar: Drop clip inside, hold the magnet underneath, and see if you can move the clip.
- Shoe: Put the magnet in the toe, and see if it will hold the clip through any surface.

VIII. Procedure
1. Using the activity sheets, discuss the *Key Question:* "Through which materials will a magnet attract a paper clip?"
2. Students predict by writing *yes* or *no* in the *My Guess* column.
3. Test each item with a magnet, and record results.
4. Have groups share their test results with the whole class. Repeat parts of the investigation when test results differ.
5. Provide an exploratory time for groups to exchange magnets, materials, or testing strategies.
6. Group objects into two sets, those through which the magnet could attract the clip, and those through which it could not. Discuss the characteristics of the materials in each group.

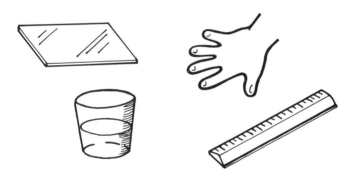

IX. Discussion
1. Through which materials can you attract and move the clip?
2. What happens when you change the position of the magnet or the materials?
3. Why did some students get different results with the same materials? What was different?
4. How did your results compare with your predictions?
5. How could you test an object for magnetic properties? (Use the smallest possible portion of the material with the strongest available magnet, analyze object for known magnetic and nonmagnetic materials.)
6. Through which kinds of materials did the magnet attract the clip? Through which kinds didn't it attract?

X. Extensions
1. Starting with a material through which the magnet can attract, have students change the conditions so that the magnetic attaction can no longer be observed. (Try more layers of the materials, a weaker magnet, a heavier object,

adding a magnetic material for a barrier, or holding the object at a greater distance.)
2. *Rescue the Paper Clip:* Drop a paper clip into a glass of water. Challenge students to remove the clip from the glass without spilling the water. The solution is to use a magnet, holding it outside the glass near the clip until the two interact; then slowly move the magnet and clip up the side of the glass until the clip *jumps* onto the magnet.

XI. Curriculum Correlations
Language arts: Have students each write one sentence about magnetism. Correct them, and have students copy each on a strip of oaktag. Arrange some of them on the floor to form a report. Use repeated ideas for a second or third report. Post reports on walls or bulletin board. Have students tape record them, to be played at your next Open House.

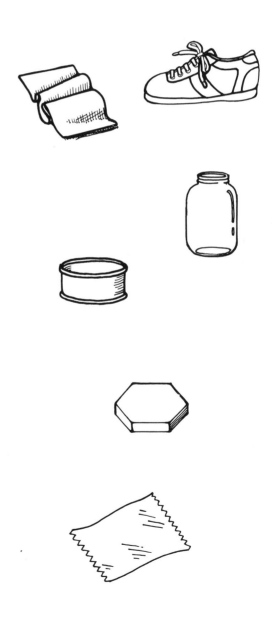

Name _____

Will a Magnet Attract Through These?

My guess — Test Results

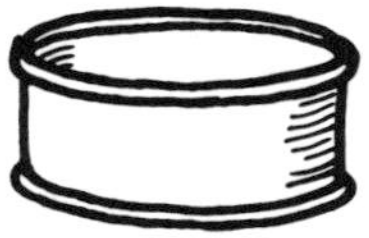

tin can

aluminum foil

shoe

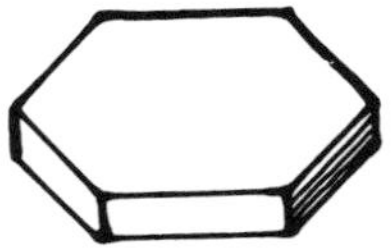

pattern block

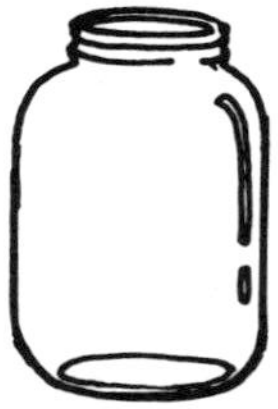

glass jar

My guess — Test Results

wooden ruler

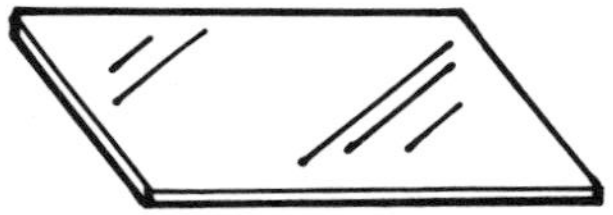

cardboard

water

hand

piece of fabric

Through It All

I. Science Topic Area Physical science: magnetism, magnetic interaction through paper

Math Topic Area Using number sense & numeration

II. Introductory Statement
Students will investigate and measure through how many pieces of paper a magnet can maintain observable magnetic interaction with a paper clip.

III. Math Content

Using number sense & numeration
Using whole number operations

Science Processing Skills

Observing
Making hypotheses
Identifying & controlling variables
Reporting data
Interpreting data

IV. Materials
For the class:
Overhead transparency or poster of *Class Chart*

For each group:
Magnet
Ruler
Tape
Paper clip
Telephone book, catalog, or other book with numbered pages.

V. Key Question
Through how many pages will a magnet attract a paper clip?

VI. Background Information
A *magnetic field* is the space around a magnet in which there is a concentration of magnetic force. Magnetic fields are strongest near the north-seeking and south-seeking poles. Magnetic fields can pass through both magnetic and nonmagnetic materials. This can be demonstrated by placing a thin barrier such as a piece of paper between a magnet and a small magnetic object; the magnet's attractive force should be readily observable. If, however, the magnet is too weak, the barrier too thick, or the magnetic object too massive, the effects of the magnet's attraction may not be observable even though the magnetic field is still

present. See *Science Information*, beginning on page 92.

VII. Management
1. Students should work in groups.
2. Newspaper can also be used, but the pieces would have to be counted.
3. Beforehand, tape the magnet on top of one end of the ruler.
4. The purpose of starting with page one is to eliminate the counting of pages. Instead, you may wish to challenge student groups to work out their own strategies. *If you do use page numbers, remember that you must divide by two to allow for the two sides to each page.*
5. Number magnets to facilitate recording data on the *Class Chart* and for doing other whole class activities. Catalogs may also be numbered if appropriate.

VIII. Procedure
1. Discuss the *Key Question:* "Through how many pieces of paper will a magnet attract a paper clip?" Share ideas for finding out.
2. Students record a prediction on the activity sheet, then draw their magnets (complete with numbers), and their catalogs.

3. Open each catalog to page one.
4. Place the magnet on the left hand page, turn one page, and place the clip on top of the magnet, so that by moving the ruler you move the clip.
5. Continue to turn pages and move the clip until the clip will no longer move by moving the magnet. Turn back to the last page on which the clip will move.
6. Count pages or note page number and divide by two (because each page has two

sides). Record the number of pages through which the magnet will move the clip.

7. As groups find and record the greatest number of pages, have them also record data on the *Class Chart*: the numbers of their magnets, the number or description of their catalogs, and the greatest number of pages through which their magnets attracted.

8. With the whole class, share observations about the data. Guide students to make observations about the relationships among the various group results. Record this data analysis in the *Notes* column. Help them to realize that the data differ because various elements of the investigation differed: magnets, clips, catalogs, and strategies used.

9. Have students fill in the last part of the activity sheet in their own words, telling why group data differed.

IX. Discussion

1. How should you decide on a reasonable prediction? What do you already know about magnets that should help you?
2. What difference would magnet strength make?
3. Does the paper of pages in various catalogs differ? Did anyone use the cover of the catalog as one page? What influence would that have on results?
4. Are there any results you would like to retest?
5. Which catalog/magnet/clip combination had the greatest number of pages?

X. Extensions

1. Average the *Number of Pages* column.
2. Using the *Class Chart* as a reference, let students test other combinations of catalogs, magnets, and clips. Record on a second *Class Chart*.

3. Make a list of things students could change to increase the number of pages. Try at least some of them.
4. Use one catalog to test all magnets, or use one magnet to test all catalogs. What difference did it make? Why would this be an appropriate scientific procedure?
5. Put magnets in order by their demonstrated strength.

XI. Curriculum Correlations

Language arts: Have students write a *syntu* poem about a magnet. Syntu is a form of unrhymed poetry with five lines; syllables are not counted:
Line 1. Name the object.
Line 2. Describe the object.
Line 3. Give an emotional reaction to the object (like, dislike, what it makes you think of, etc.)
Line 4. Give another description of the object
Line 5. Give another name for the object

An example:
Ring of mine
Small and gray and heavy
Exciting and magical
Makes things move and jump
My special friend

XII. Home Link

Work as a class to find the combination of catalog, magnet, and style of paper clip which yields the greatest possible number of pages. (This is preferable to making it competitive.) Allow other catalogs, magnets, and clips to be brought from home. Invite parents or friends to the *finals*.

Through It All

Names _____

_____

_____

_____

Through how many pages will a magnet attract a paper clip ?

Our guess:_____ pages

Test result: _____ pages

My Catalog

My Magnet

We learned that_____

_____

_____

Through It All

	Magnet Number	Telephone Book, Catalog, etc.	Number of Pages	Comments
Group 1				
Group 2				
Group 3				
Group 4				
Group 5				
Group 6				
Group 7				

HOW CLOSE CAN YOU GET?

I. Science Topic Area — Physical science: magnetism, quantifying magnetic interaction

Math Topic Area — Measuring length

II. Introductory Statement

Students will quantify the level of observable magnetic interaction between a magnet and a paper clip, and then will quantify the increase when the second and third magnet units are added to the first.

III. Math Content

Using number sense & numeration
Measuring length

Science Processing Skills

Observing
Making & testing hypotheses
Reporting data
Interpreting data

IV. Materials

For each pair of students:
3 similar magnets
1 paper clip

V. Key Question

How close to a paper clip does a magnet have to be before the clip moves toward the magnet?

VI. Background Information

In this investigation we are really dealing with two variables, the number of magnet units and the distance between the magnet(s) and the object. First we must establish a baseline by determining at what distance a paper clip will move toward a single unit magnet, and then we can investigate what happens when we increase the number of magnet units.

When two magnets are joined with unlike poles together, they become one combined magnetic force and are considered one magnet. Such a *2-unit magnet* will be stronger than one magnet but not quite as strong as the combined strength of the two magnets tested separately. If additional magnets are added, the increment will be less each time. See *Science Information* beginning on page 92 for additional information.

VII. Management

1. Students should work in pairs.
2. For most reliable data, be sure to have the paper clips just barely touching the ruler and magnets exactly perpendicular to the table. When two or three are used, they must all touch the table.

VIII. Procedure

1. Distribute magnets and activity sheets.
2. Ask the *Key Question:* "How close to a paper clip does a magnet have to be before the clip moves toward the magnet?"
3. Write predictions (for a 1-unit magnet only) on activity sheets.
4. Decide which person will move the magnet and which will watch the clip to see when it moves.
5. Place the magnet and paper clip on the activity sheet.
6. Move the magnet slowly and evenly toward the clip. Let students practice once or twice, so that they can hold it still and take an accurate measurement whenever the clip moves. When the clip does move, note the distance as *Trial 1*.
7. Do three trials with a 1-unit magnet, noting test results in the appropriate boxes.
8. Average the three trials, and express it in both centimeters and millimeters.
9. Compare results as a class. Discuss any results that are considerably different from the rest of the class. Why are they different?
10. Repeat with one 2-unit and then one 3-unit magnet.

IX. Discussion

1. Does it make a difference which end of the magnet is facing the magnet?
2. What is happening as you move the magnet toward the paper clip, *before the clip moves*?
3. Why are we experimenting three times and then averaging the results? Did you get nearly the same result each time?
4. How many millimeters are there in a centimeter?
5. Did your predictions improve with the 2-unit and 3-unit magnets?
6. What pattern did you see as you added the second and third magnet units? What do you think would happen with a fourth or fifth one?

X. Extensions

1. Repeat the investigation with any of these variations:
   - placing magnet(s) flat instead of on edge
   - students exchanging magnets
   - changing clip so that the *double end* is in reversed position
   - using customary units of measure instead of metric
   - continuing to add magnet units beyond three
   - substituting a large paper clip
   - substituting a smaller magnet and nudging it toward the clip without holding it
2. Have students make up a game, using the phenomenon of paper clip often jumping toward the hole of the ring magnet. For example, you might glue a small paper point on the clip, and then see who can get it exactly in the hole.

XI. Curriculum Correlations

Language arts: Make a list of words that describe all the ways a paper clip can move: jumping, snapping, sliding, etc.

XII. Home Link

Send a letter home to locate an adult who can speak to the class about a subject related to magnets: engineering, computer technology, small appliance repair, geology, etc.

Name _____

HOW CLOSE CAN YOU GET?

What effect will the number of magnets have?

	1 magnet	One 2-unit magnet	One 3-unit magnet
My guess			
Trial 1			
Trial 2			
Trial 3			
Total			
Average	____cm or ____mm	____cm or ____mm	____cm or ____mm

Summary: _____

_____

WHAT ON EARTH IS A COW MAGNET?

Level 1

Cows have a problem. They like to eat hay and grain. Often there are short pieces of wire mixed in with their feed. When they swallow the feed, they also swallow many of these bits of wire.

If the wire stays mixed with the feed, there is no problem. Other times, however, some of the wires get caught in the cow's stomach. This can hurt the cow.

Veterinarians or "vets" are animal doctors. They use a special tube to put a cow magnet into the back of each cow's mouth. The cow swallows the magnet easily because of its shape. It is long, narrow, and round, something like a thick crayon.

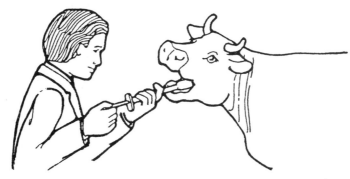

Since the magnet is heavy, it sinks to the bottom of the cow's stomach. As the wire bits go into the stomach, they stick to the magnet instead of hurting the cow. One magnet can help a cow for her whole life. If cows could talk, do you think they would thank the vets for giving them the cow magnets?

WHAT ON EARTH IS A COW MAGNET?

Level 2 Page 1

Magnets come in many shapes and sizes, but the cow magnet was invented to solve a very serious problem of dairy farmers. To understand how cow magnets help, it is necessary to know how a cow's stomach works.

As you might guess, a cow has a very large stomach. In an adult cow it can hold about 280 liters (over 60 gallons) of food. The stomach is divided into four compartments: the rumen, the reticulum, the omasum, and the abomasum.

The muscles in the walls of the rumen and reticulum mix and moisten the food. Then it is passed back up into the mouth, where the cow chews it thoroughly. We say the cow is "chewing her cud". Then the food is swallowed a second time. This time it passes through all four sections of the stomach and on to the rest of the digestive system.

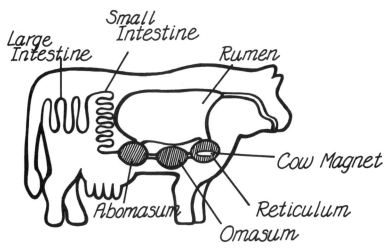

Highly schematic drawing of a cow's digestive system

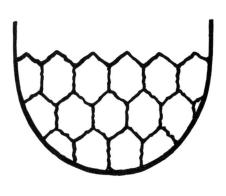

Close-up of honeycomb cells of reticulum

When we start to eat food with a seed or a piece of bone in it, we usually feel it in our mouths before we swallow it. Cows, on the other hand, swallow their food so quickly the first time that they do not sort out the small bits of hay wire and other scrap that gets into their food. As a result, they swallow many of these bits of wire.

If the wire stays with the food, there is no problem, but unfortunately the wire often becomes lodged in the honeycomb-like hexagonal cells of the mucous membrane in the cow's reticulum or second stomach. The motion of the cow causes some of the wires to go through the walls of the cow's digestive tract and sometimes even into its heart.

Veterinarians use a special tube to put a cow magnet in the back of a cow's mouth. The cow swallows the magnet easily because it is long, narrow, and round, something like a thick, smooth, heavy crayon. Since the magnet is heavy, it sinks to the bottom of the rumen. As wire bits go into the rumen, they stick to the magnet instead of the stomach lining. One small cow magnet can help a cow for her whole life.

Mining With Magnets

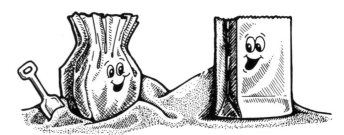

I. Science Topic Area
Physical science: magnetism, magnetic materials in soil

Math Topic Area
Comparing & measuring masses

II. Introductory Statement
Students will use a magnet to obtain iron bits from sand and then from other soil; then, they will compare these two quantities to see which is a better source of iron bits.

III. Math Content
Measuring mass
Using whole number operations
Identifying & using inequalities

Science Processing Skills
Observing
Making & testing hypotheses
Classifying & sorting
Identifying & controlling variables
Reporting data
Interpreting data

IV. Materials
For each pair or group:
Part 1:
Magnet
Pint carton of sand
Cup of water
Paper towels
2 plastic lock-type bags, labelled *sand* and *soil*.

Part 2: Above supplies plus
Pint carton of soil
Balance scale & gram masses
1 plastic lock-type plastic bag (to find mass when empty)

V. Key Question
Is there any iron in sand?
Is there more iron in sand or in other soil?

VI. Background Information
Soil is found on the top layer of the earth's surface. It is made up of mineral particles mixed with animal and vegetable matter. The mineral particles are found in three size categories: sand, silt, and clay. What we commonly refer to as *sand* is usually large size particles without much humus (the animal and vegetable matter). In this investigation, sand and soil will be referred to as two different materials, because of the visual difference and also the disparity in the amounts of magnetic materials they contain.

Magnetic material is found in observable quantities in beach sand and commercial play sand (sold for children's sand boxes). Soil with humus contains less magnetic material proportionately. The magnetic particles in all types of soil consist mostly of magnetite, plus some ilmenite and a very few micrometeorites; there is sufficient iron content in all of these to be attracted by magnets of moderate strength. See *Science Information* beginning on page 92 for more information.

VII. Management
1. Students work in pairs or in small groups.
2. If you plan to use both *Parts 1 and 2*, set a time limit on mining for both sand and soil; try 3 minutes. Allow ample time for *Part 1*, because students will mine iron bits more quickly in sand, and when they mine in soil they will need a longer time to gather a measurable amount of iron bits.
3. Be sure to save the iron bits for other investigations.
4. The strength of magnets and the type of sand and soil used are crucial. Cow type (bar) magnets work best. Test magnets beforehand with various types of sand and soil to familiarize yourself with the process.
5. Since the iron bits tend to cling to magnets, they gather inside the hole of ceramic ring magnets. Enclosing them in plastic wrap may help, but the plastic tends to tear when the magnets are used to mine in the soil. Placing them in an inside out plastic sandwich bag will result in mining fewer iron bits but will keep the iron bits from clinging. For these reasons, many teachers prefer to use other shapes of magnets.

VIII. Procedure
Part 1
1. Ask the first *Key Question:* "Is there any iron in sand?" and help them write their predictions.
2. Discuss how we could find out. Have students share what they know about mining. Explain the class will be mining, but using magnets

instead of explosives, picks, or shovels!

3. Distribute sand or take students to wherever they will be *mining*.
4. Have them move the magnets in the sand for the stated time or until they have an accumulation of materials on their magnets. (See #2 in *Management*.)
5. Dip the magnets into water, and rub to eliminate all nonmagnetic materials.
6. Using small pieces of paper towel, remove iron bits from the magnets in bunches.
7. Lay pieces of towel out so that iron bits are exposed to the air (to minimize rusting). Bright sunshine will dry them quickly, but beware of breezes!
8. Discuss what the particles may be. Have students note any rust. Guide students to realize that since magnets attract mainly iron, what was attracted must be magnetic and probably all or mostly iron.

Part 2

1. Ask the second *Key Question*: "Is there more iron in sand or in other soil?" Guide students to realize that magnets pick up materials containing iron, and that by putting a magnet in sand or soil, we can see if it picks up anything.
2. Have students note their predictions on the activity sheet.
3. Mine for iron bits as in *Level 1*. Place bits in the *soil* bag. (The answer to the *Key Question* may be obvious at this time, but students should be encouraged to wait and compare the two portions of iron bits on a balance scale *to be sure*.)
4. Let all bits dry overnight or for several hours in bright sunlight.
5. Measure the mass of an empty bag, then *sand* and *soil* bags. Fill in information on the activity sheet. If necessary, combine iron bits from several groups or even from the whole class. Record class total. (With younger students, the two bags may simply be placed in the balance scale to see which side has the greater mass.)
6. Discuss what is in the bags. (Since a magnet was used, they must be magnetic particles.)
7. Compare results with predictions.

IX. Discussion

1. When we move the magnet in the sand or soil, what happens?

2. When we put the magnet in water, what falls away from it? Why did we use water? What if we had done it without water?
3. What was it that the magnet attracted in both sand and soil? (magnetic particles, mostly iron)
4. Why were the iron bits difficult to remove from the magnet? Did anyone try to reuse a piece of paper towel? What happened?
5. What would happen if we put the iron bits into the plastic bags without drying them thoroughly? (rust) Why? What does this prove about the bag contents?
6. Do you think other samples of sand and soil might give us different results? Why?

X. Extensions

1. Measure the mass of both portions of iron bits.
2. Examine the iron bits with a magnifier. Discuss the different sizes and types of particles, and that a few may be micrometeorites!
3. Dry the nonmagnetic materials and examine them also. How is the nonmagnetic sand different from the nonmagnetic soil? List what you found (including hair, sticks, etc.) Explain that sand refers to the size of the particles, that it is also soil (see *Background Information*).
4. Determine the percentage by mass of iron bits to all sand and soil (including magnetic and nonmagnetic particles).
5. Repeat the investigation using sand and soil from different locations.
6. Have a treasure hunt with students delving for washers, clips, dull nails, etc. in boxes of soil or sand, using only magnets.
7. When bits have dried and been put into bags, hold a magnet near the bag. Why aren't all the bits attracted? (Some may have clung to magnetic bits when damp; there may also have been some induced—temporary—magnetism.)

XI. Curriculum Correlations

Language arts/spelling: Learn the definitions and spelling for words used: sand, soil, iron, mine, magnet, mass, magnetic, balance.
Social studies: Learn more about various types of mining, especially iron mining. Make a map of areas in which iron is found and mined. Study the effect of mining on the environment. A good source is the *National Geographic Magazine*, but reading level may be too high. For bulletin boards, trim pictures, mount, and add a simplified commentary.

XII Home Link

Have students bring in sample cartons of soil from their yards. Set up an interest center where students can mine for iron bits. Be sure cartons are labeled with students' names, and that each box is mined for the same period of time. Tape the plastic bag with iron bits from each sample to the container or to a bulletin board display.

Mining With Magnets

Part 1

Is there any iron in sand?

I think _____

Here's how to find out.

You will need:
  a magnet
  some sand
  a cup of water
  paper towels

1. Rub a magnet in some sand.

2. Wash off the nonmagnetic materials.

3. What is left on the magnet?

4. Take the iron bits off the magnet, using small pieces of paper towel.

5. Let them dry overnight.

6. Put them in a plastic lock-type bag for safe keeping.

I discovered _____

_____

Mining With Magnets

Part 2

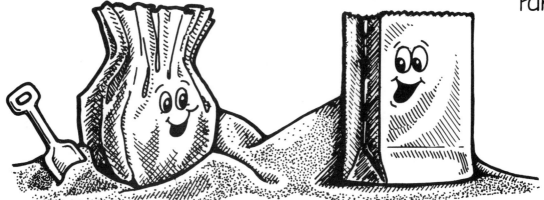

Is there more iron in sand or in other soil?

Mass of sand bag   _____ gm

Mass of empty bag   _____ gm

_____

Mass of iron bits from sand   _____ gm

Mass of soil bag   _____ gm

Mass of empty bag   _____ gm

_____

Mass of iron bits from soil   _____ gm

We found more iron bits in _____.

Why? _____

_____

_____

      48

Magnetic Lines

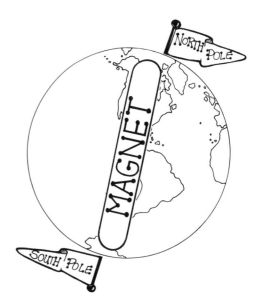

I. Science Topic Area — Physical science: magnetism, magnetic field lines

Math Topic Area — Using geometry and spatial sense

II. Introductory Statement
Students will discover the magnetic field lines of magnets, and then will illustrate the earth's magnetic field lines using a map and a magnet, and iron bits.

III. Math Content

Using geometry & spatial sense

Science Processing Skills

Observing
Making & testing hypotheses
Collecting & organizing data
Reporting data
Interpreting data

IV. Materials
Part 1:
Variety of magnets (bar, ring, horseshoe, etc.)
Iron bits (See *Mining with Magnets*)
Paper cups for shakers
Overhead transparencies (or white paper)
Optional:
    Clear varnish or fixative spray
    Overhead projector

Part 2:
Bar magnets (preferably not cow type)
Iron bits
Paper cup for shakers

V. Key Questions
Where are the magnetic field lines of a magnet?
How is the earth like a giant magnet?

VI. Background Information
A magnetic field exists in the magnet and in the space around it. The magnetic field is strongest near its poles. The shape of a magnet's magnetic field is shown by the magnetic field lines that spread out from both poles and meet in a series of extended arcs.

The earth acts as if there were a large bar magnet running from north to south through the middle of it. Actually, the magnetic north pole is not at the earth's geographic north pole; it moves constantly, and there is evidence that it has even traded places with the south magnetic pole a number of times. At present (1991), it is located near Bathurst Island, north of mainland Canada, about 1,000 miles from the geographic North pole, and is moving at the rate of about fifteen miles per year. See *Science Information* beginning on page 92.

VII. Management
1. Students should work in small groups.
2. Prepare the cup shaker by punching two or three small holes in the bottom with a pencil.
3. CAUTION: If using spray, follow directions carefully.
4. For *Part 2*, it is best if the length of the magnets is the same as the diameter of the earth on the activity sheet; if this is not possible, substitute plain circles with appropriate diameters for the activity sheet globe.
5. Although it is less effective, you may place a plastic sandwich bag with iron bits on top of the paper and magnet, instead of sprinkling the iron bits. Rubbing two pieces of steel wool together above the magnet will also reveal the lines.

VIII. Procedure

Part 1

1. Have each team place a magnet on the table, and then lay the transparency over it, with the magnet near the center.
2. Pour the iron bits into the cup while covering the holes, or else hold the cup over the transparency.
3. Move the cup as you *very gently* sprinkle the iron bits onto the transparency, so that the magnetic field lines are revealed. If you intend to spray any projects, try to sprinkle a minimum of iron bits on the perimeter of the magnet because a thicker layer of iron bits will not be anchored to the transparency by the varnish spray.
4. Spray varnish, first from a distance of about two feet, then more closely, moving all over the whole surface. Use extra spray on thicker accumulations of iron bits at the perimeter of the magnet.
5. On the activity sheet, students should draw their group's magnet and magnet field lines.

Part 2

1. Place the bar magnet on the table, with the activity sheet map on top of it.
2. Sprinkle iron bits on the paper until the magnetic field lines are revealed.
3. Discuss the patterns that are revealed. Explain that the earth does have magnetic north and south poles and also a magnetic field something like what they see.
4. Repeat this activity (several times if necessary) until students realize that the magnetic lines do not fall in the same locations each time. Explain that the magnetic field exists in this whole area, and that even between the lines there is magnetic force.

IX. Discussion

1. How would you describe the pattern formed by the iron bits? Where are the lines closest together? What do you think this means?
2. Where are more iron bits concentrated? Where are there fewer?
3. What do the magnetic field lines show?
4. Which part of the magnet do you think has the strongest magnetic power?
5. Which part of the earth has the strongest magnetic power?

X. Extensions

1. Have students repeat the investigation with a magnet of a different shape, either on the activity sheet or on another piece of paper.
2. Repeat the investigation using pairs of magnets side by side. Try it first with unlike poles together; use a second pair for like poles. Are the patterns different?
3. Substitute blueprint paper for the transparency. When the magnetic field lines are formed, place the whole thing in the sun for 3-5 minutes. Bring the paper in, shake off the iron bits, and rinse the paper in water.

XI. Curriculum Correlations

Social studies: Find out more about Bathurst Island and the area near the magnetic north pole.
Language arts: Do library research on the use of magnetic fields for directional orientation by homing pigeons and even by some people!
Language arts: As a class think of ten sentences giving facts about magnetic fields and magnetic field lines.

Magnetic Lines

Part 1

Where are the magnetic field lines of a magnet ?

1. Place a magnet on the table.
2. Put the plastic on top of the magnet.
3. Sprinkle iron bits on top.
4. Tap the plastic gently.
5. Draw what you see..

Where did most of the iron bits go ? _____

Geologist _____

Magnetic Lines

How is the earth like a giant magnet? Part 2

1. Place this map of the earth on top of a bar magnet, under a line from the north to the south pole.
2. Put plastic on top of the map.
3. <u>Slowly</u> sprinkle iron bits over the top of the map.

What do you see? _____

_____

What did you learn? _____

_____

Face To Face

I. Science Topic Area
Physical science:
magnetism,
magnetic poles

II. Introductory Statement
Students use pairs of magnets to discover how like and unlike poles react to one another.

III. Science Processing Skills
Observing
Making & testing hypotheses
Identifying & controlling variables
Reporting data
Interpreting data

IV. Materials
For the class:
2 sheets 12 x 18" red construction paper
2 sheets 12 x 18" blue construction paper
Red and blue materials for preparing magnets (masking tape with felt marker dots, colored plastic tape, filing dots, or tempera paint)

For each pair of students:
2 or more ring magnets (See *Management*)

V. Key Question
What happens when two magnets get close to each other?

VI. Background Information
The areas of a magnet where magnetic force is most concentrated are its poles. Magnets usually have two poles, north-seeking and south-seeking. If two magnets are placed side by side with like magnetic poles together, they will repel one another; if unlike poles are together, they will attract. See *Science Information* beginning on page 92.

VII. Management
1. Students should work in pairs, but with guided whole class discussions throughout the lesson.
2. Beforehand, prepare the magnets:
   a. Mark one side of a (test) magnet *red*, the other side *blue*. (For purposes of this lesson, it does not matter which pole is which color.)
   b. Mark a second magnet by holding it close to the red side of the test magnet; the side needed that is attracted to red should be marked blue because it must be the opposite pole.
   c. Mark the other side of this magnet red.
   d. Mark all the other magnets in the same way.
3. As a visual aid, prepare two large paper *magnets*. Cut out large magnet shapes, two red and two blue; paste one of each color together to form two magnets each with a red and a blue side.
4. During *Part 1*, be sure to allow time for students to think through and explain their predictions so that they develop *predicting* as a processing skill.

VIII. Procedure
Part 1
1. Begin as a whole group without magnets. Ask the *Key Question*: "What happens when two magnets get close together?" Does it matter which sides of the magnets are facing one another?
2. Guide students to think of the four ways in which two magnets could be put together: red face to red, red to blue, blue to red, and blue to blue (plus touching edges!)
3. Establish appropriate vocabulary: *interact, like, unlike, attract, repel, move together,* and *move apart*.
4. On the activity sheet, color the pictures of magnets for Trial 1. Have students predict what will happen.
5. Distribute magnets and have students actually hold the magnets with red faces together. Circle the picture that tells what happened. Did the magnets attract each other or repel?
6. Continue with the other trials in the same way. Encourage students to refer to the two faces of magnets as poles.
7. Guide students to see the pattern, that if like poles (colors) are face to face, they will repel one another; if unlike poles are face to face, they will attract.

Part 2
1. Set aside all magnets. Using the activity sheet, discuss and predict how the magnets

53

should be stacked. Color the magnets accordingly.

2. Distribute magnets and use them to find out *what worked.*
3. Record results by coloring magnets.

IX. Discussion

1. What happens when the red faces get close to one another? Will they want to move together or apart? What about the other combinations?
2. Does it matter if you put blue to red or red to blue?
3. Why do you think the magnets push or pull when they are put together differently? What is happening?
4. Did everyone in the class have the same test results?
5. What words can we substitute for *red* and *blue*? (*same* and *different*)
6. In stacking the three magnets, what is the pattern you see? Did everyone have the same answer for what worked? How did results compare with predictions?

XI. Curriculum Correlations

Creative writing: Have students apply another definition of *magnetic* by writing stories titled "My Magnetic Personality," in which they describe things they say or do that they think attract other people. (When they finish and share these, remind them that magnets both attract and repel; they might want to think about things they do and say that repel others!)

X. Extensions

1. Try the same activity with bar magnets, color-coding the ends.
2. Remove tape or paint from magnets. (Take care to dry them thoroughly if you wash paint off to avoid rusting.) Explore the way they attract and repel one another. Let students relabel them.
3. Lay two magnets flat on the table, side by side, with edges touching. How does this change the action of the magnets? Does it matter which sides are up when you do this?

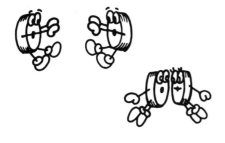

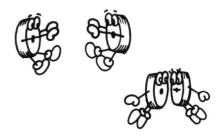

Scientist_____   Part 1

Face To Face

1. Predict and circle your guess.
2. Move magnets "face to face".
3. Circle your results.

Trials	My Guess	Results
red **red**		
red **blue**		
blue **red**		
blue **blue**		

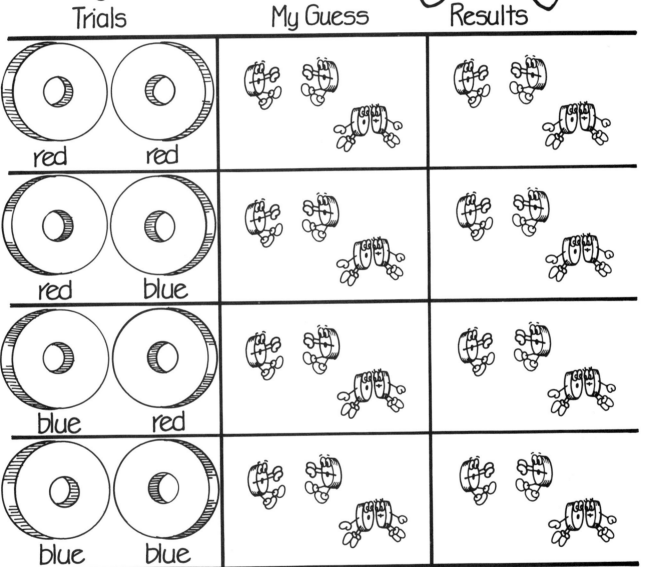

Brenda Howsepian

Here is what I found out.

A _____ magnet a _____ magnet.
  (color)   (color)

A _____ magnet   a _____ magnet.
  (color)   (color)

Stacking Magnets

How should we stack magnets so they will stay together?

Make your guess by coloring these magnets red or blue.

My guess

What worked

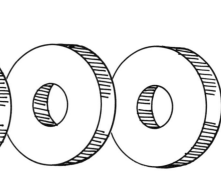

What pattern do you see?

HUNGRY HOUNDS

I. Science Topic Area

Physical science:
magnetism,
magnetic poles,
magnetic interaction

II. Introductory Statement

Students will move paper dogs along a path by pushing or pulling with a magnet.

III. Science Processing Skills

Observing
Identifying & controlling variables
Making & testing hypotheses
Interpreting data

IV. Materials

For each student:
2 magnets
Ruler
Tape
Paper clip

V. Key Question

How can you make an object move using a magnet?

VI. Background Information

This investigation applies two basic characteristics of magnets, the attraction/repulsion of their poles and their ability to interact with magnetic objects through many materials. Every magnet has a magnetic field which is strongest at its poles. The poles of a ring magnet are on its large, flat sides. If two magnets are placed *facing* each other with like magnetic poles together, they will repel one another; if unlike poles are together, they will attract. Magnetic fields are able to pass through many materials, demonstrated by placing a thin barrier, such as a piece of paper, between a magnet and a paper clip or between two magnets. Note that the magnet can only attract the clip, but two magnets can either attract or repulse one another. Attraction and repulsion would seem to be two types of magnetic force, but such is not the case. They are really two manifestations of a single magnetic force. See *Science Information* beginning on page 92.

VII. Management

1. Tape each magnet to the end of a rule, as shown.

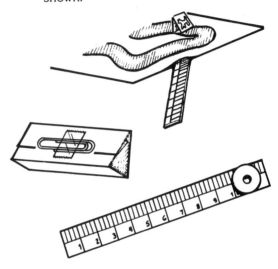

2. Assemble *Hungry Hounds* by taping or pasting tabs. (Use separate tape for clips, so they can be replaced by magnets for repelling.)
3. Keep it an exploratory activity, rather than a competitive one. Avoid races.

VIII. Procedure

1. Distribute *hungry hounds* and activity sheets. Assemble hounds, but do not distribute magnets or attach paper clips yet.
2. Ask the *Key Question*: "How can you make an object move with a magnet?" How could you make the *hungry hound* move down the path to the bone using a magnet?
3. Attach paper clips to tabs on hounds, and distribute rulers with magnets.
4. Pull each hound along the path by placing the ruler under the track, so that the hound is on top of the magnet with the paper between.
5. Ask students how they could *push* the hound. Replace the paper clip with a magnet. Check that the downward face of this magnet *repels* the upper face of the ruler magnet.
6. Push the hounds down the path (or try)!
7. Let students share what they observed.

IX Discussion

1. What are two ways you can move an object? (pull or push)

2. Was it easier to push or pull the hound down the path? Why?
3. What else could we have used besides a paper clip?
4. What would happen if we turned over the hound's magnet?

X. Extensions

1. Have students design other objects and tracks, such as a rabbit and a path to some carrots or a boat with water path.
2. Draw a larger set of paths on newsprint and use a meter stick instead of the ruler.
3. For more practice in visual-motor coordination, make and activity sheet with a path that grows narrower as it approaches the bone, or try a race with two straight paths and two magnets taped on one ruler, set to repel.
4. Have students try other barriers besides the paper. (table, book, chair)

XI. Curriculum Correlations

Math/reading: Divide the path into blocks, with a number problem or vocabulary word in each block. Call a word or the answer to one of the problems, and have students move the hound (or whatever) to that block.

Art: Build a sculpture by placing a magnet on the table and arranging magnetic objects on top of it. Make it permanent by gluing the objects together, or let students reuse objects by doing it in an interest center.

XII. Home Link

Encourage students and their families to watch for newspaper and magazine articles about magnets. Paste these clippings in a big scrapbook. Good sources are catalogs and also magazines like *Popular Mechanics*.

HUNGRY HOUNDS

Start Here

59

FLOATING MAGNETS

I. Science Topic Area
Physical science: magnetism, magnetic poles

Math Topic Area
Measuring length

II. Introductory Statement
Students will experiment with two or more stacked ring magnets, observing how they interact with one another.

III. Math Content
Measuring length

Science Processing Skills
Observing
Making & testing hypotheses
Identifying & controlling variables
Reporting data
Interpreting data

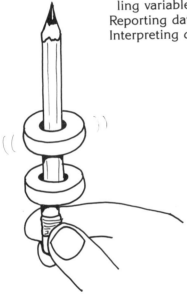

IV. Materials
For each group:
Pencils
Ring magnets, at least 1 per person
Optional clay

V. Key Question
What would happen if you put two ring magnets on an upright pencil?

VI. Background Information
Each magnet has a magnetic field, with the strongest magnetic force at its poles. Normal magnets have two poles; in industry or research they may have more but usually an even number. If two magnets are placed *facing* each other with like magnetic poles together, they will repel; if unlike poles are together, they will attract. Ring magnets have one pole on each flat side. See *Science Information* beginning on page 92.

VII. Management
1. Students should work in cooperative learning groups so that they can combine their magnets for explorations.
2. The optional clay would be used as a base for pencils to add stability.

VIII. Procedure
1. Ask the *Key Question:* "What would happen if you put two ring magnets on an upright pencil?"
2. Students discuss their predictions.
3. Provide time for students to investigate with two magnets for each pencil. How close were predictions to what actually happened? On activity sheets draw magnets attracting and repelling each other.
4. Encourage students to fill their pencils with floating magnets, and then draw what happens on the activity sheet.
5. Encourage students to arrange various numbers of magnets in various ways. What patterns do you see in the behavior of the magnets and the spaces?

IX. Discussion
1. Why does the magnet float on one side and not on the other?
2. Where is the north-seeking pole on a ring magnet? . . . the south-seeking pole?
3. What would happen if the pencil weren't there?
4. What happens to the spaces between magnets as you add more?
5. Can you make the magnets bounce?
6. How can you make the top magnet jump off the pencil?

X. Extensions
1. Using a long dowel, float all available magnets from the whole class.
2. Measure (metrically or in customary units) the space between floating magnets with one magnet and then with more magnets on top. What is the pattern?
3. Have students create a *labor-saving invention* which makes use of floating magnets.
4. Make a *piston* using several floating magnets in a plastic pill container. (You can also use a 35 mm film container, but use at least 4 magnets or line it with a thick piece of paper, something to prevent magnets from flipping over.)
5. Try stacking 2, 3, or 4 magnets in different patterns of attracting and repelling.

XI. Curriculum Correlations

Creative writing/music: Have students write words for a song, *I'm Foreveer Floating Magnets* (instead of "I'm Forever Blowing Bubbles").

Art: Design and build a *dancing puppet* for your pencil. Draw a figure at least 6 cm wide and 10 cm tall, leaving 1 cm across the bottom for a base. Cut with paper double, so you will have a back. Color the back as the back of the doll. Fold bases forward. Staple or glue top and sides of doll together, but leave base and bottom center open. Tape or glue bases of doll to a magnet. Put 1 magnet on the pencil with pole upward which repels the doll magnet. Place doll magnet on top. make the doll *dance* by jiggling the pencil (and bottom magnet) up and down.

FLOATING MAGNETS

Try it: Make two magnets stick together on your pencils.

Try it: Make two magnets float on your pencil.

Try it: Fill your pencil with floating magnets.

Draw a picture of what you did.

Now try this: Using what you have learned, make a magnet pop off your pencil. How did you do it?

     © 1991 AIMS Education Foundation

I. Science Topic Area
Physical science: magnetism, relating magnetism to gravity

II. Introductory Statement
This is a creative, open-ended activity in which students use magnets and other materials to build systems that defy gravity.

III. Science Processing Skills
Observing
Making & testing hypotheses
Identifying & controlling variables
Reporting data
Interpreting data

IV. Materials
For each group:
Magnets, large number of strong ones
Tape
String
Paper clip
Steel soup can (unopened)
Additional items such as pins, pencils, rulers, plastic film canisters, cylindrical pill boxes, wire, scissors

V. Key Question
How can you devise a system that defies gravity?

VI. Background Information
Forces cause things to move. We are familiar with mechanical forces: kicking a ball, lifting a book, or hammering a nail. In mechanical force, direct contact is required. There are other forces in the universe, however, that are even more fundamental and do not require direct contact. In physics, the major forces are usually considered to be gravity, electromagnetism, the strong nuclear force, and the weak nuclear force. Each of these forces can move something by pushing or pulling on it without touching it.

Of these four major types of force, gravity is probably the one with which we are most familiar. We all know that if we jump up, we will be pulled back to earth by gravity. It is also true that the same gravity that holds us so tenaciously in its grip also holds the planets in their orbits. As a result of our familiarity with gravity, we tend to think of gravity as a very strong force. In reality, however, gravity is the weakest of the four fundamental forces; any of the other three could be used to defy or over-

come it. For example, the magnetic force holding a magnet on the refrigerator is stronger than the gravitational force pulling it toward the floor.

Gravity and magnetism are alike in some respects and quite different in others. Gravity is similar to magnetism in that it is an interaction between two objects. We do not usually think of our pulling on the earth as the earth pulls on us, but that is exactly what happens. Gravity is defferent from magnetism in that it only attracts, whereas a magnet can both attract and repel another magnet. See *Science Information* beginning on page 92.

VII. Management
1. Students should work in small groups where they can share ideas and learn to work together as they build their gravity defying systems.
2. Groups should be encouraged to be creative, so that they develop as many systems as possible. All systems designed by students should be recognized as acceptable, however, as long as each group can explain how gravity is being defied.
3. Since this activity is designed to be open-ended, have available a large number of magnets and as wide as possible a variety of materials.

VIII. Procedure
1. Remind students of the activity in which they floated magnets on a pencil, and discuss the principles involved. Explain that *defy* means to *go against*.
2. Have each group build the gravity defying system pictured on the activity sheet. Place the magnet at the top of the soup can.
3. After tying the clip at one end of the string, tape the other end to the table.
4. Position the can so that the clip and the magnet are attracted to one another and yet do not touch. Discuss how this system uses magnetism to defy gravity. (Gravity would make the clip fall to the table; instead, it is held in the air by magnetism.)
5. Challenge students to think of other ways to defy gravity using a magnet. Show them what materials are available.
6. Have each group work together to build at least one system that defies gravity. Praise groups that are creative.
7. Have students draw and describe how their

64

systems work. If a group creates more than one system, have them choose one to tell about.

8. Help the class to form a group conclusion all can use on their activity sheets. (Tell what would happen if the magnet weren't there, and then when it is there.)

IX. Discussion

1. Why does the clip seem to float in air? What would happen if the string were not taped down?
2. Which is stronger, the pull of the earth's gravity or the pull of the magnet?
3. What is gravity? What effect does gravity have on us? . . .on falling objects? . . .on airplanes taking off and landing? . . .on objects attracting each other magnetically?
4. What did all of the successful gravity defying systems have in common?

X. Extensions

1. Move the can closer to and farther away from the paper clip. What happens?
2. Experiment with different barriers between the clip and the can: various types of paper, foil, etc.
3. Try putting the magnet on other parts of the can. Substitute other magnetic objects for the can or the paper clip. What characteristics must the object and the magnet have?
4. Find out about some applications of this gravity defying ability of magnets. (friction-less bearings, magnetic flotation beds, etc.)

XI. Curriculum Correlations

Language arts: Think of an invention using magnets to defy gravity, and write a patent for your invention. (Look up *patent* if necessary.)
Reading: Read about *superconductors* and their ability to defy gravity.

DEFYING GRAVITY

How can you devise a system that defies gravity?

Try This:

Build the system pictured by using a tin can, ring magnet, paper clip, string and tape.

How does it defy gravity?

Challenge:

Work together with your group to build other systems that defy gravity.

Draw a picture of one of your systems.

Describe how your system works.

_____
_____
_____
_____
_____
_____
_____
_____

I learned _____
_____
_____

Magnetic TUG OF WAR

I. Science Topic Area Physical science: magnetism, magnetic poles

Math Topic Area Measuring length

II. Introductory Statement
Students will quantify magnetic interaction between two ring magnets to find out the mathematical relationship between attraction and repulsion.

III. Math Content

Math Content	Science Processing Skills
Measuring length	Observing
Using whole number operations	Making & testing hypotheses
Averaging	Identifying & controlling variables
	Reporting data
	Interpreting data

IV. Materials
For each pair of students:
2 ring magnets

V. Key Question
Between two magnets, which is stronger, the push or the pull?

VI. Background Information
Most magnets have two poles. If two magnets are placed with like magnetic poles together (both north-seeking or both south-seeking), they will repel one another; if unlike poles are together, they will attract. The mathematically measured magnitude of attraction and repulsion is always equal, although other factors such as friction or gravity may make this difficult to prove precisely. See *Science Information* beginning on page 92.

VII. Management
1. Students work well in pairs, with one controlling the magnets and the other observing the measurement.
2. Students need a familiarity with the attraction and repulsion of magnets before doing this investigation. Use AIMS lessons *Face to Face, Floating Magnets, Hungry Hounds,* or a time of free exploration to provide this experience.

VIII. Procedure
1. Ask the *Key Question:* "Between two magnets, which is stronger, the push or the pull?"
2. Discuss possible answers, and guide students to give reasons for the predictions they write on the activity sheets.
3. Explain that we are going to try to find the answer by measuring how close one magnet must be to another before the other one moves. Make clear that any movement at all counts.
4. Review, if necessary, how to read the metric scale shown.
5. To use activity sheets, be sure to have a level surface. (With more advanced students, use a level to check.) Place one magnet (Magnet A) on either flat side on top of the outline.
6. Place the other (Magnet B) flat beside A. Test to find the side on which they *attract* each other.
7. Place Magnet B on its outline at the right.
8. Holding only Magnet B, move it slowly and steadily toward A. When A moves, stop moving B and mark the place. Record this measurement beside *Trial 1.*
9. Repeat for Trials 2 and 3. Total and average these measurements.
10. Turn Magnet B over, and check that they now repel one another.
11. Using the lower half of the activity sheet, test the magnets on edge in the same way, first for attraction and then for repulsion. Note results and average them, as before.
12. Discuss what happened. Guide students to write a conclusion, either individually or as a class.

IX. Discussion
1. Why do magnets attract or repel one another? What is magnetic interaction.
2. What is a magnetic pole? How many does a magnet have? Where are they on a ring magnet?
3. Why did we have three trials each time?
4. How accurately did you predict what would happen?
5. How did Magnet A move when it was flat?
6. How do your results for attraction compare with those for repulsion? What pattern do you see?
7. How did the magnet move when it was on edge?

8. Why were the three trials different from one another?

9. What was happening to the magnets' domains from the time you started moving Magnet B until your Magnet A moved? (An increasing number of domains were becoming aligned.) Were the magnets interacting before A moved? (yes, but not enough to be observed)

10. What seems to be the mathematical relationship between attraction and repulsion? How would you explain any results that don't fit this pattern?

X. Extensions

1. Measure in customary units or in different metric units (millimeters if you used centimeters, for example).
2. Try the investigation using magnets on edge but have edges facing one another.
3. Have students exchange mgnets or use a different type of magnet.
4. Make bar graphs of the averages.
5. Have students discuss whether or not there would be a way to use horsehoe magnets for this activity.

XI. Curriculum Correlations

Language arts: Although attraction and repulsion are not really opposing forces, the two magnets do move in opposite directions. Discuss and apply the concept of *opposites*. Use some opposite pairs of words as reading or spelling words. Play a game in which you give a word and the student gives a word meaning the opposite: Push-pull, give-take, black-white, up-down, deposit-withdraw, sunrise-sunset, etc. Be sure they understand that there can sometimes be more than one word that is the opposite of another.

XII. Home Link

Play a game with someone at home. Quietly start doing an action which is the opposite of the other person's action: sitting down instead of standing up, holding hands together instead of apart, opening mouth instead of closing it, etc. Do this until the other person catches on to what you are doing. Be sure to stop if it becomes annoying!

Magnetic TUG OF WAR

Between two magnets, which is stronger, a magnet's push or its pull ? I predict _____

centimeters

| 1 | 2 | 3 | 4 | 5 | 6 | 7 | 8 | 9 | 10 |

Place Magnet A here

Slide Magnet B ← this way

Pull

	Distance apart when A moves
Trial 1	
Trial 2	
Trial 3	
Total	
Average	

Push

	Distance apart when A moves
Trial 1	
Trial 2	
Trial 3	
Total	
Average	

centimeters

| 1 | 2 | 3 | 4 | 5 | 6 | 7 | 8 | 9 | 10 |

Place Magnet A here →

Slide Magnet B ← this way

Pull

	Distance apart when A moves
Trial 1	
Trial 2	
Trial 3	
Total	
Average	

Push

	Distance apart when A moves
Trial 1	
Trial 2	
Trial 3	
Total	
Average	

Now I think _____

69

HOW DO MAGNETS LOSE POWER?

Magnetic materials can be magnetized or made into magnets. They can also be demagnetized and lose their power. All magnets become weaker gradually over time. This is called aging. There are other ways they become weaker, either suddenly or gradually.

Electromagnets are demagnetized each time the electric power is turned off. This is useful because we want to control them. When we tell an electromagnet to magnetize, it will lift heavy objects made of magnetic material. When we tell it to demagnetize, it will drop or let go of the objects. Electromagnets are made so that they gain or lose magnetic power when we press the right buttons. When they lose power, they are doing exactly what we want them to do.

Hitting or dropping magnets can strengthen or weaken them, depending on where it happens. In a STRONG magnetic field (near a strong magnet, for example), tapping iron or steel can help to align the domains and magnetize them. On the other hand, if magnets

are dropped or hit in a WEAK magnetic field (away from magnets), they will lose some of their magnetism.

To keep magnets strong, we should try not to drop them or hit them against anything.

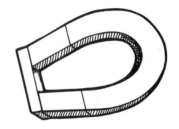

To keep magnets strong, it is important to store them properly. Always place them so that their opposite poles are together. They should attract one another, not repel. Each horseshoe magnet should be stored with a keeper, a piece of soft (pure) iron across its ends or poles.

> If we are careful
> not to drop or hit our magnets,
> they will stay strong for a long time.

Making Magnets

I. Science Topic Area
Physical science:
magnetism,
making magnets

Math Topic Area
Graphing

II. Introductory Statement
Students will magnetize scissors and then will use staples to quantify the magnetic strength of the magnets they have made.

III. Math Content
Using number sense
& numeration
Using set theory
Graphing

Science Processing Skills
Observing
Making & testing
hypotheses
Collecting & organiz-
ing data
Identifying & control-
ling variables
Reporting data
Interpreting data

IV. Materials
For each group:
2 pr. small school scissors
Magnet (moderately strong)
Staples, at leat 30 per magnet
2 empty cans to store staples

V. Key Question
How can you make a magnet?

VI. Background Information
Iron and other magnetic materials are made up of very small areas called *magnetic domains*. Each domain consists of billions of atoms. The atoms within each individual domain are always perfectly aligned toward magnetic north. In contrast, the domains themselves may or may not be aligned. Current research indicates that the domains pointing in the right direction probably become larger at the expense of those pointing in other directions.

How do the iron's domains know which way to align themselves? Since opposites attract, touching or stroking the iron with the south-seeking pole of a magnet will make that end of the iron the north-seeking pole, and the domains facing in a north-seeking direction will be the ones to grow. If only a few domains become aligned, the object will become slightly magnetic; if most of the domains become aligned, the material will be strongly magnetic. No material ever has all of its domains aligned.

The amount of magnetic strength a magnet has depends on several factors such as the material from which it was made and the strength of the magnet that magnetized it. Magnets are often classified in two groups, permanent and temporary, according to how strong they are and how well they retain their magnetism. For more information see *Science Information* beginning on page 92.

VII. Management
1. This activity is appropriate for cooperative learning groups.
2. Small, inexpensive school scissors are recommended for this lesson. They will magnetize easily, but they will also demagnetize easily so you can repeat the investigation. This activity is often done using nails, but unless strong magnets are used, the nails will not be magnetized enough to attract many staples and make the appropriate bar graph.
3. CAUTION: Keep magnets, scissors, and staples separate from each other before and after you use each of them. Keep unused staples in one can, and take out only what you need each time.
4. Beforehand, test all scissors for magnetism by trying to pick up staples with them. If they are slightly magnetic they can still be used for this activity. Some sewing scissors have been magnetized purposely during manufacture (for picking up pins) and will be unsuitable. Hitting weakly magnetic scissors against one another should demagnetize them.
5. Since much contact is desired between magnet and magnetic material, stroke on the flat (blade) surface of the scissors, always at the same end of the scissors.
6. One stroke consists of a movement in one direction only. *If you stroke back and forth, each direction counts as one stroke.*
7. There is some difference of opinion, even among authorities, about whether the

magnet strokes should be made in one or both directions. In *Part 1*, the students stroke in one direction; then in *Part 2*, they stroke in both directions and compare results of the two strategies.

8. During the lesson, check that students do not hold the magnet on the scissors *while* they pick up staples. If the number of staples is unusually high, this may be the reason!

9. If you think a staple has some induced magnetism, test it by trying to pick up other staples with it.

10. Separate staples easily by loading them into a stapler and dispensing them.

VIII. Procedure

Part 1

1. Demonstrate how few—if any—staples the scissors will attract. Ask the *Key Question*: "How can you make a magnet?"

2. Distribute staples in cans, then scissors, magnets, and activity sheets.

3. Have students try to pick up some staples with the scissors. Discuss how many staples the scissors attracted, and record in the *0 strokes* box on the activity sheet.

4. Stroke the scissors blade in one direction with the same pole of the magnet 10 times and immediately test to see how many staples it will attract. Record results and set aside magnetized staples.

5. Stroke 20, 30, 40, and 50 times in the same way, testing and recording results each time.

6. Discuss with the class what happened as they stroked the scissors more and more. What pattern do they see?

Part 2
Decide which level activity sheet to use.

Level 1

1. Ask the students, "Which makes a stronger magnet, stroking in one direction or stroking it back and forth in both directions?"

2. On the bar graph for *Part 2*, fill in data on stroking in one direction from *Part 1*.

3. To demagnify the scissors, hit two pairs together several times. Check with staples that they are demagnified.

4. Magnetize the scissors again, but this time stroke in both directions *without lifting the magnet*. Count each direction as a stroke.

5. Fill in the second bar graph.

6. Guide students to compare their own pairs of bar graphs, to decide if they think the method is important. Do all students agree on the conclusion? To resolve any difference, redo part or all of the investigation.

Level 2
Follow the same general procedure using the *Level 2* activity sheet. Guide students as they explain their predictions, plan their bar graphs, and label both axes. In the class discussion, allow ample time for sharing observations and developing possible reasons for different results. Encourage students to wait until they have shared observations with the whole class before writing their conclusions.

IX. Discussion

1. Why didn't the scissors and the staples interact at the beginning?

2. What is a magnet?

3. Why was it important to set the staples aside while we stroked the scissors?

4. What happened to the number of staples attracted as we stroked the scissors more? Why?

5. Why shouldn't you count staples that are hooked onto other staples? (may not be attracted magnetically) What could you do with staples that are hooked onto others?

6. When you stroke in one direction, why is it important to lift the magnet before the next stroke?

X. Extensions

1. Magnetize the scissors another way, by stroking one pole to one point of the magnet on scissor and then the other pole on the other point. You should get opposite polarity on the two points. Explore the implications. For example, do the scissors pick up more staples with points separated or together? Does it matter if you stroke one or both directions?

2. Try magnetizing other magnetic objects, such as a metal ruler, large nail, darning needle, crochet hook, or a large jar top.

3. For *Part 2*, compile a class summary on a transparency made from the activity sheet. Total and average data on both methods.

XI. Curriculum Correlations

Language arts: Do a simulation of making a magnet using several student groups. Outline large rectangles on the floor, and let students help decide how to dramatize what really happens. You might have several stand in each rectangle to represent domains in bars of iron, for example. Students could represent magnets, paper clips, and so on.

Language arts: Write a paragraph describing a magnet; include what it can do and how to take care of it.

Making Magnets

Part 1

Names _____

_____

_____

_____

How can you make a magnet ?

Try to pick up staples with a pair of scissors. Record how many staples you get in the 0 strokes box. Do the scissors act like a magnet ? _____

2. Stroke the scissors 10 times in one direction. How many staples will the scissors attract ? Record.

3. Stroke the scissors 10 more times, Test and record for 20 strokes.

4. Stroke the scissors 10 more times. Test and record for 30 strokes.

5. Continue stroking, testing, and recording in the same way for 40 and 50 strokes.

50 strokes	
40 strokes	
30 strokes	
20 strokes	
10 strokes	
0 strokes	

What did you observe ?

_____

_____

_____

Making Magnets

Professor

Part 2 Level 1

Which makes a stronger magnet, stroking in one direction or in both directions?

My predictions: _____

	10	20	30	40	50
10	⊏	⊏	⊏	⊏	⊏
9	⊏	⊏	⊏	⊏	⊏
8	⊏	⊏	⊏	⊏	⊏
7	⊏	⊏	⊏	⊏	⊏
6	⊏	⊏	⊏	⊏	⊏
5	⊏	⊏	⊏	⊏	⊏
4	⊏	⊏	⊏	⊏	⊏
3	⊏	⊏	⊏	⊏	⊏
2	⊏	⊏	⊏	⊏	⊏
1	⊏	⊏	⊏	⊏	⊏

0 10 20 30 40 50

Number of Strokes – One Direction

	10	20	30	40	50
10	⊏	⊏	⊏	⊏	⊏
9	⊏	⊏	⊏	⊏	⊏
8	⊏	⊏	⊏	⊏	⊏
7	⊏	⊏	⊏	⊏	⊏
6	⊏	⊏	⊏	⊏	⊏
5	⊏	⊏	⊏	⊏	⊏
4	⊏	⊏	⊏	⊏	⊏
3	⊏	⊏	⊏	⊏	⊏
2	⊏	⊏	⊏	⊏	⊏
1	⊏	⊏	⊏	⊏	⊏

0 10 20 30 40 50

Number of Strokes – Both Directions

I found out _____

MOSTLY MAGNETS

75

© 1991 AIMS Education Foundation

Making Magnets

Part 2 Level 2

Prediction: Which makes a stronger magnet, stroking in one direction or stroking in both directions.

_____

Explain your prediction: _____

_____

_____

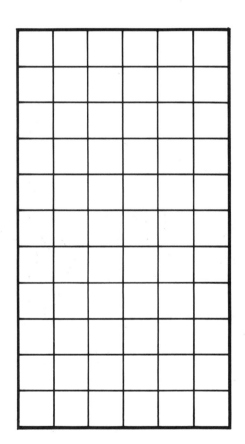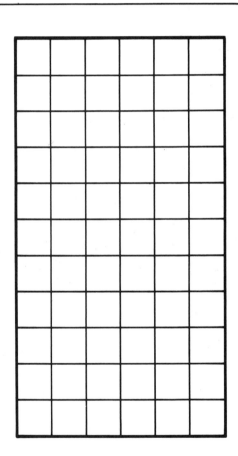

Conclusions: _____

_____

_____

_____

76   © 1991 AIMS Education Foundation

Make A Compass

I. Science Topic Area
Physical science: magnetism, magnetic compasses

Math Topic Area — Using spatial sense

II. Introductory Statement
Students will construct a magnetic compass with a magnetized needle.

III. Math Content
Using spatial sense

Science Processing Skills
Observing
Identifying & controlling variables
Reporting data
Interpreting data

IV. Materials
For each compass:
Large steel needle (preferably darning or dull crewel type)
Square, flat piece of styrofoam, from meat tray (each side about 3 cm)
Magnet
Plastic bag with iron bits or staples
Glass pie plate
Water
Optional: red nail polish

V. Key Question
How can you make a compass?

VI. Background Information
The compass is an old and well-known instrument used to determine directions. It was the first practical use for magnetism. Long ago, mariners could use familiar shore landmarks to guide them. As they sailed out of sight of land, they utilized the stars and other natural phenomena. They couldn't see the stars on cloudy or stormy nights, however, just when they needed them most. Because of such problems, the earliest magnetic compass was welcomed, especially for use on longer voyages. (The instrument is also called a *directional* or *navigational* compass.) See *Science Information*, beginning on page 92.

VII. Management
1. Students should work in groups, but preferably each person should make a compass.
2. The dish must be made of glass, aluminum, or some other nonmagnetic material. It must have a smooth surface and enough space for the floating needle to pivot freely without surface tension pulling it to the side. (Some think a bit of liquid detergent diminishes the surface tension effect.)
3. Pins may be used instead of needles if they are not too small for students to handle; they are less expensive and work well.
4. When you have magnetized a needle, it will point magnetic north and south, but you won't know which end is pointing north. There are at least two practical solutions. One way is based on knowing which pole you used to stroke the needle. Since opposite poles attract, the north-seeking pole of a magnet would cause the end stroked to become the south-seeking pole, which would *seek* the *south* magnetic pole! If, on the other hand, you do not know which pole you used, you can locate south by observing which end of the needle points to the portion of the horizon where the sun is during the day. (Of course, you could also check with another compass, but that seems to us a bit like cheating!)

VIII. Procedure
1. Ask students to point in the direction they think is *north.* Discuss how they decided. Guide the discussion to establish that using a magnetic compass would be a more reliable method.
2. Ask the *Key Question*: "How can you make a compass?"
3. Show that an unmagnetized needle does not point in any direction consistently. Magnetize a sewing needle by stroking it with one pole of a magnet 40-50 times or for about one minute. Check it has been magnetized by holding it near the plastic bag with iron bits or staples.
4. *Put away all magnets now, since they can interfere with the functioning of the compasses.*
5. Put the needle half way through the styrofoam diagonally, as shown.
6. Place the needle and styrofoam in the middle of the dish, and add just enough water so that the tip of the needle pivots while barely touching the bottom of the dish. Add or subtract water until the needle touches the bottom and turns freely.
7. Rotate the floating needle slightly in the center of the dish. It should come to rest with the

needle ends pointing to magnetic north and south. Students should record their observations on the activity sheets.

8. Turn the needle in another direction. (It should return to the same position as before.) Record observations.

9. Discuss how we can determine which of the two ends is pointing north. (See #4 in *Management*.) Students may wish to turn their styrofoam over if the upward tip of the needle points southward. (Once the north-seeking end has been identified, it may be dipped in red nail polish.)

10. Place compass on the circle on the activity sheet.

11. Turn the paper so that *north* is below where the needle is pointing north.

12. Using their compasses, have students label where the other three directions are on the activity sheet. If appropriate for your group, explain that the compasses are pointing toward magnetic rather than geographical north.

IX. Discussion

1. How did we make the compass? Give the steps in order.

2. What causes the needle to point to the north magnetic pole?

3. What would happen if we put a magnet near a compass? (Try it!)

4. How is this compass like the kind you buy in a camping store? How is it different?

5. How does the needle of a camping compass stay in the middle of a compass without water? (center stem)

6. Why wouldn't these compasses work well on ships out on the ocean? How could we improve them?

7. Why couldn't we use a steel bowl instead of the glass dish?

X. Extensions

1. To make the compasses more suitable for later use and for use at home, have students use the activity sheet to label the *dish* with the four cardinal compass points.

2. Check directions on the compasses made with a commercially made compass. How accurate are the compasses the students made?

3. Practice following a compass. Have students give commands to each other, such as "Go east one meter" and "Go south three meters."

4. Add intercardinal points (northeast, southeast, etc.)

5. Identify and label the position of cardinal and intercardinal points in terms of degrees:
    North: 0 or 360 degrees
    Northeast: 45 degrees
    East: 90 degrees
    Southeast: 135 degrees
    South: 180 degrees
    Southwest: 225 degrees
    West: 270 degrees
    Northwest: 315 degrees

6. Encourage students to invent other directional compasses, such as hanging a bar magnet on a string or suspending a straightened bobby pin in a jar of oil.

XI. Curriculum Correlations

Social studies: Examine local and world maps. How do these maps indicate north? Make a simple map of the classroom, indicating the cardinal compass points in a corner.

Language arts: Discuss the various meanings for the word *compass*. Use the dictionary. Have students make up some sentences in which it is unclear which kind of compass is meant. ("He used his compass in math class.") Think of ways to make the meaning clear. (might use words *magnetic* or *directional*)

XII. Home Link

Parents, brothers, and sisters will enjoy seeing the compasses made at school. Be sure to shield needles in compasses being taken home.

Make A C🧭mpass

Navigator

1. Magnetize a needle by stroking it.

2. Push the needle halfway through a piece of styrofoam at an angle.

3. Put the needle in a flat dish.

4. Pour in a little water until the needle turns.

5. What happens ?_____

_____

6. Turn the needle. What happens ?_____

_____

7. Place the dish on the circle. Turn the paper until the needle lines up with the north and south lines.

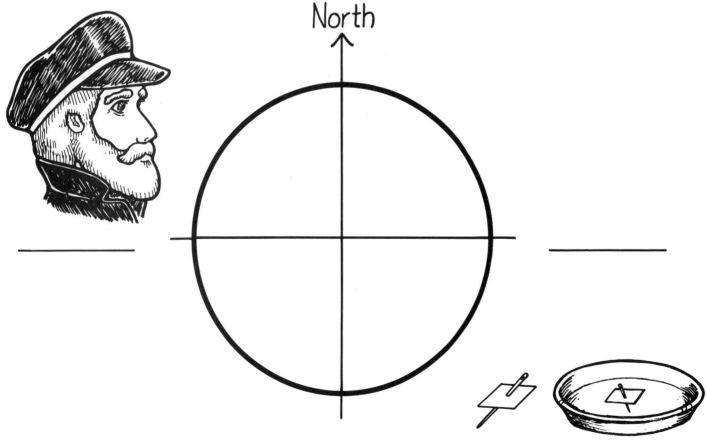

North

You made a compass ! _____

Make An Electromagnet

It will help to have a partner!

You will need
- *1 nail about 8cm (3in.) long*
- *40 cm magnet (or other insulated) wire*
- *size D battery*
- *staples or other small magnetic items*

To make your electromagnet
1. *Wind the wire tightly around the nail, leaving 10 cm free at both ends.*
2. *Remove the insulation at both ends of the wire.*
3. *One partner holds the ends of the wire firmly on the bottom and tip of the battery.*
4. *The other partner tests the nail electromagnet by picking up the staples with the nail.*

See if any of these will make your magnet stronger:
- *Push together or pull apart the coil of wire.*
- *Wind more of the wire on the nail.*
- *Try someone else's battery or nail.*
- *Try longer or shorter pieces of wire.*
- *Experiment with different sizes of batteries or nails.*
- *Try 2 batteries or 2 nails.*
- *Other ideas _____*

What increased the power? _____

_____

What decreased the power? _____

_____

What would you use to build a large electromagnet powerful enough to pick up junk cars and other scrap metal?

_____

What's the Attraction?

I. Science Topic Area
Physical science: magnetism, magnetic attraction, and repulsion

II. Introductory Statement
Students will determine the average force of magnetic interaction (attraction and repulsion), measured in newtons, with magnets composed of a varying number of ring magnet units.

III. Math Content
Measuring force in newtons
Averaging
Computing percent of error
Graphing, using tables

Science Processing Skills
Observing
Making & testing hypotheses
Collecting & organizing data
Reporting data
Interpreting data

IV. Materials
For each group:
Spring scale, preferably marked in newtons (can be in grams as noted in *Background Information*)
4 ring magnets
2 paper clip stems with magnets (see Fact Sheet *Instructions for Building Paper Clip Stems*)

V. Key Question
How do magnetic attraction and repulsion compare mathematically?

VI. Background Information
When two or more ring magnets are joined, the composite is considered a single magnet. In this lesson we make a distinction between a composite magnet and the ring magnet units with which it is formed.

A *newton* (N) is a unit measuring force. It is the amount of force which, acting upon one kilogram of matter, will give it an acceleration of one meter per second for every second the force acts. If a scale is marked in grams (instead of newtons), the results can be approximated in newtons by dividing by 100. Note that the abbreviation is a capital letter, but the unabbreviated form is written in lower case.

Attraction and repulsion would seem to be two types of magnetic force, but such is not the case. They are really two manifestations of a single magnetic force which we know as *magnetic interation*. Two magnets attract or repel each other because their magnetic fields are in a certain orientation, a specific spatial position, with either like or unlike poles together. If unlike poles are together, the magnets will attract each other; if like poles are together, they will repel. Although the mathematically measured magnitudes of these two orientations are always equal, factors such as friction or gravity may prevent this fact from being proven precisely in the classroom.

In this activity the term *pull* is used as a synonym for *attraction* and *push* for *repulsion*. For more information on magnetism, see *Science Information* beginning on page 92.

Prior to the first series of tests, students can only guess what the tests results will be. However, after the first set of three tests have been completed and the average computed, students are in a position to make a more informed guess or *prediction* for subsequent tests. This sequence provides an occasion to discuss the difference between a *guess* and a *prediction*. A *guess* grows into a *prediction* when there is some relevant evidence.

The *absolute value* of a number is its real value without regard to whether it is positive or negative. Another way to define *absolute value* is as the number of units of the number *n* from zero on a number line. Thus, $|+3|=3$ (read "the absolute value of positive three equals three") because $+3$ is located 3 units to the right of 0, while $|-3|=3$ since -3 is located 3 units to the left of 0.

The *percent of error* is a way of representing the difference (or lack of it) between two measures. In this investigation, it will show how close the prediction (P) is to the average test result (A).

$$\text{percent of error} = \frac{|P-A|}{A}$$

For example, if the prediction (P) is 3 and the average test result (A) is 5,

$$\% \text{ of error} = \frac{|3\cdot5|}{5} = \frac{|\cdot2|}{5} = \frac{2}{5} = 40\%$$

VII. Management

1. Students should work in cooperative learning groups. If equipment is limited, rotate groups through a lab center.
2. This investigation requires great care in reading the spring scales at the times of maximum attraction and repulsion. This takes place instantaneously, so the scale must be watched closely to catch the reading. An environment in which students can concentrate is essential.

VIII. Procedure

Page 1
1. Assign roles to group members, preferably one to handle the apparatus, one to record, and at least two to observe the apparatus.
2. Using the apparatus with spring scale and two paper clip stems with magnets to demonstrate, discuss the question given on the activity sheet: "How much force is needed to pull these magnet sets apart or push them together?
3. Students guess how many newtons it will take to pull two magnets apart.

Pull or Attraction
(See Fact Sheet *Instructions for Using Paper Clip Stems*)
4. For the *Pull* section, place Magnet X (with 1 magnet) on the scale hook. Hold Magnet Y (with 1 magnet) so that it is attracted to and touching Magnet X. Hold scale and magnets horizontally to minimize the effects of gravity.

5. Pull the scale and Magnet X in one direction and Magnet Y in the other until they separate. Have students watching to read the scale when this happens. Record as Trial 1.
6. Repeat and record for Trials 2 and 3. Total the trials, average them, and compute the *percent of error* (see *Background Information*).
7. For the second set of trials, make predictions as before. Demonstrate that they will add a second magnet to Magnet X by adding the second magnet unit over the paper clip stem so that this second magnet unit is attracted to the first.
8. Test predictions as before and record results.
9. Continue the rest of the *Pull* section as indicated on the activity sheet.

Push or Repulsion
(Set aside the paper clip stem used as Magnet Y in the activity above. In this part of the investigation, Magnet Y will be the magnets placed over the stem of Magnet X so that they repel Magnet X. Pull the scale with one hand and with the other pull on Set Y as shown on the Fact Sheet.)
10. Make predictions for one magnet unit repelling one magnet unit. Test predictions, record trial results, total, average, and compute the *percent of error*.
11. To add the second magnet unit to Magnet X, remove the repelling magnet and place a magnet (either this one reversed or another) so it is attracted to the Magnet X magnet. Then place a repelling magnet on the stem. Continue with the trials and the remainder of the *Push* section on Page 1.

Page 2
1. As a class, discuss the range of data as recorded on Page 1. Do this by finding out the lowest and highest number of newtons recorded for either attraction or repulsion. Set the scale to include both of these; it will vary according to various factors, especially the strength of magnets. Students fill in the scale across the bottom of the graph. Remember that the scale must begin at zero.
2. Fill in the graph by groups, using group test results.
3. Ask students to record any significant observations. These may relate either to the relative strengths of magnets or the comparison of attraction and repulsion.

VIII. Discussion

1. What is magnetic interaction?
2. Are attraction and repulsion two different forces or different orientations of the same force? What do we mean by *orientation*?
3. How does the force of attraction compare mathematically with the force of repulsion?
4. What effect does increasing the number of ring magnet units have on the power of a composite magnet?

IX. Extensions

1. Use a transparency to record a class summary.
2. Increase the number of ring magnets forming the composite magnets and continue with the investigation.
3. Test whether other groups' individual ring magnets have the same magnetic force of attraction.

XI. Curriculum Correlations

Language arts: Double check the students' understanding of the terms *newton* and *percent of error*. Have several rephrase definitions and give illustrations applying the terms. Include work in dictionaries, encyclopedias, and trade books.

Art/oral language: Have students draw the apparatus in the two positions and explain the investigation.

What's the Attraction?

How much force is needed to pull these magnet sets apart or push them together?

% of error $\dfrac{|P-A|}{A}$

_____

_____

_____

Names

Record of Attraction or Pull

Ring Magnets in Magnet X	Magnet Y	P GUESS/ PREDICTION	TRIAL 1	TRIAL 2	TRIAL 3	TOTAL	A AVERAGE	% OF ERROR
1	1							
2	1							
2	2							
3	1							
3	2							
3	3							

Record of Repulsion or Push

Ring Magnets in Magnet X	Magnet Y	P GUESS/ PREDICTION	TRIAL 1	TRIAL 2	TRIAL 3	TOTAL	A AVERAGE	% OF ERROR
1	1							
2	1							
2	2							
3	1							
3	2							
3	3							

What's The Attraction?

Name _____

Which requires more force, to pull these magnets apart or push them together?

Newtons Of Force

Ring Magnets in Magnet Magnet X Y	Type																
1 1	PULL																
	PUSH																
2 1	PULL																
	PUSH																
2 2	PULL																
	PUSH																
3 1	PULL																
	PUSH																
3 2	PULL																
	PUSH																
3 3	PULL																
	PUSH																

Number of Newtons _____

Observations: _____

_____

MOSTLY MAGNETS   85

INSTRUCTIONS FOR BUILDING PAPER CLIP STEMS

Step 1: Use scotch tape to seal off one end of the center hole in the magnet.

Step 2: Open a small paper clip as shown and crimp one end of the clip to form a right angle.

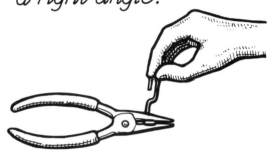

Step 3: Insert the crimped end of the paper clip into the center hole of the magnet.

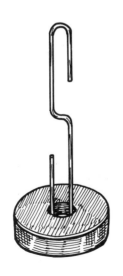

Step 4:

Using a glue gun, fill the center hole. Avoid having the glue cover any part of the top side of the magnet.

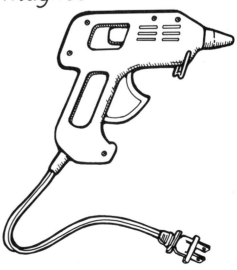

INSTRUCTIONS FOR USING PAPER CLIP STEMS

To test attraction, or pull, mount as many ring magnets on each paper clip stem as desired by slipping the magnets over the paper clip. Make sure that no glue separates the ring magnets. Hook the spring scale through the exposed end of one paper clip and grasp the exposed end of the second stem. Rest the apparatus on a table in a horizontal position. Pull on the spring scale until the magnets snap apart. Note and record the highest reading.

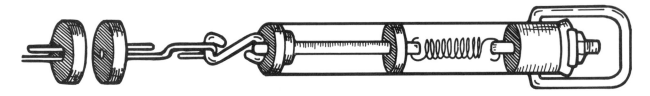

To test repulsion, or push, mount as many magnets on one paper clip stem as desired by slipping the magnets over the paper clip. Now add ring magnets in the same manner, but so they repel. If the paper clip is too short, hook a second paper clip through the first to elongate the stem. To conduct the repulsion test hold set Y with one hand. Then pull on the spring scale until the magnets just touch. Note and record the reading of the force required, indicating that the repulsion force has been counterbalanced.

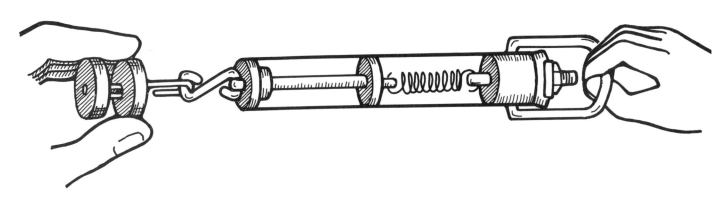

I. Science Topic Area — Physical science: magnetism, the effect of distance between magnets on magnetic interaction

II. Introductory Statement
Students will study the changes in magnetic attraction as magnets are separated by an increasing number of layers of cardstock.

III. Math Content

Measuring force in newtons
Averaging
Graphing, using tables
Using rational numbers - decimals

Science Processing Skills

Observing
Making & testing hypotheses
Collecting & organizing data
Reporting data
Interpreting data

IV. Materials
For each group:
Spring scale, preferably marked in newtons (can be in grams as noted in *Background Information*)
4 ring magnets
2 paper clip stems with ring magnets (See Fact Sheet *Instructions for Building Paper Clip Stems*)
12 pieces of cardstock or heavy paper of uniform thickness, each piece 3 cm square

V. Key Question
What is the effect on the force of attraction when the distance between two magnets is increased?

VI. Background Information
Read the *Background Information* for *What's the Attraction*. For additional information on magnetism, see *Science Information* beginning on page 92.

If scale is marked in grams rather than newtons, the results can be approximated in newtons by dividing by 100. Note that the abbreviation is a capital letter, but the unabbreviated form is written in lower case.

In this activity, the manipulated variable is the distance between the magnets, represented by the number of cardstock layers separating them. The layers aid in controlling the distance between the magnets and provide a non-standard unit of measure. It should be noted that the effect of the cardstock itself on the force of attraction is negligible and does not affect the primary result of the investigation.

With a given number of layers of cardstock, three trials are completed and averaged. Averaging provides a safeguard against serious errors in readings.

When the results are graphed, they should show an inverse relationship between the number of layers of cardstock and the number of newtons (the strength required to overcome the force of attraction). That is, the graph should demonstrate that the greater the distance apart, the less the force of attraction. Twelve trials with different distances separating the magnets will provide sufficient evidence to show this relationship. Normally, the line graph will approximate that of a smooth curve.

VII. Management
1. The class should be divided into groups and subgroups in the following way. Each group should be composed of three subgroups; each subgroup should be a cooperative learning group of 3-5 students which conducts the investigation and records data on *Page One*. Within each group, it is important to have one subgroup that uses one magnet unit each on Magnets X and Y, one subgroup that uses two magnet units each, and one that uses three. Within each group the three subgroups should choose and note three different colors. (They do not use the colors on *Page One*, but noting them there will ensure that all data will be graphed on *Page Two* in the correct colors.) Each subgroup completes the table on *Page One*. Then, each *group* works together on *one* copy of *Page Two*, graphing the results from *Page One* there in three colors. (As an example, a class of 30 students can be divided into two groups, with each group having three groups of five students. Keep in mind that to obtain accurate readings, at least two students should be assigned to watch the apparatus.)
2. If not enough spring scales are available, rotate students through a lab center.
3. Paper clip stems should be constructed at least a day ahead, so that the glue dries thoroughly. See the Fact Sheet *Instructions for Building Paper Clip Stems*.
4. Although students should have the experience of labelling the points on the vertical scale of the graph, it will be wise to experiment enough beforehand to know what an

acceptable range will be. Using no cardstock and three magnets each in composite Magnets X and Y should yield the highest reading in newtons. Use this reading for as high as possible a point on the vertical axis, so the points graphed will show as much curve as possible. Then decide what intervals will be appropriate: one tenth, two tenths, etc.

VIII. Procedure
Page One
1. Divide the class into groups and subgroups. Assign or have students choose color coding and the number of magnet units they will use. At least two students in each group should be assigned to read the spring scale to be sure they observe accurately. If at any time they get significantly different readings, the test should be repeated.
2. Remind students that *when two or more ring magnets are used to form a composite magnet, they become one magnetic force and should be considered one magnet.*
3. Working in subgroups, have students hold the apparatus as shown. With *no* cardstock between, they pull the scale and Magnet X in one direction and Magnet Y in the other. Pull directly apart rather than letting the magnets slide off one another.
4. Have students watch for the point at which the magnets separate. Note the reading on the scale. Record as Trial 1. Do this twice more, find the average of the three readings and record on the table.
5. Place one layer of cardstock between Magnets X and Y and repeat the procedure, adding one layer of cardstock at a time until the table has been completed.

Page Two
1. Each group will construct a graph. Have

students label the vertical scale of the graph according to the range of readings their three subgroups obtained (see *Management*).
2. Using the data from their *Page One* tables, subgroups take turns plotting the points and drawing connecting lines in the appropriate colors.
3. Have groups write their observations about patterns they see on the graph or other aspects of the investigation.

IX. Discussion
1. What is the relationship between the distance separating the magnets (in layers) and the force of attraction (in newtons)?
2. Could the distance separating the magnets be determined? Describe.
3. How do the results of using one, two, and three magnets to form Magnets X and Y compare?

X. Extension
Ask students to find the distance, measured in millimeters, separating the magnets at all stages of the investigation. For this they would use a sufficient number of cardstock layers to get a reasonable measure of total thickness and then divide by the number of layers. If a micrometer or vernier caliper is available, the measurements could be made more accurately. Printing establishments have instruments for measuring the thickness of paper. It might be possible to borrow one for use in this extension.

XI. Curriculum Correlation
Language arts/social studies: Use the library to explore *physics* and career opportunities of *physicists*. What does the field of physics include? What is the educational preparation of a physicist? Is there a college or university nearby with a physics department?

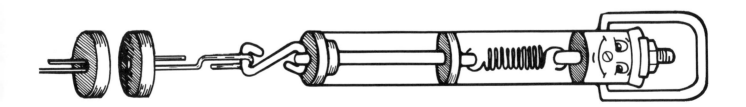

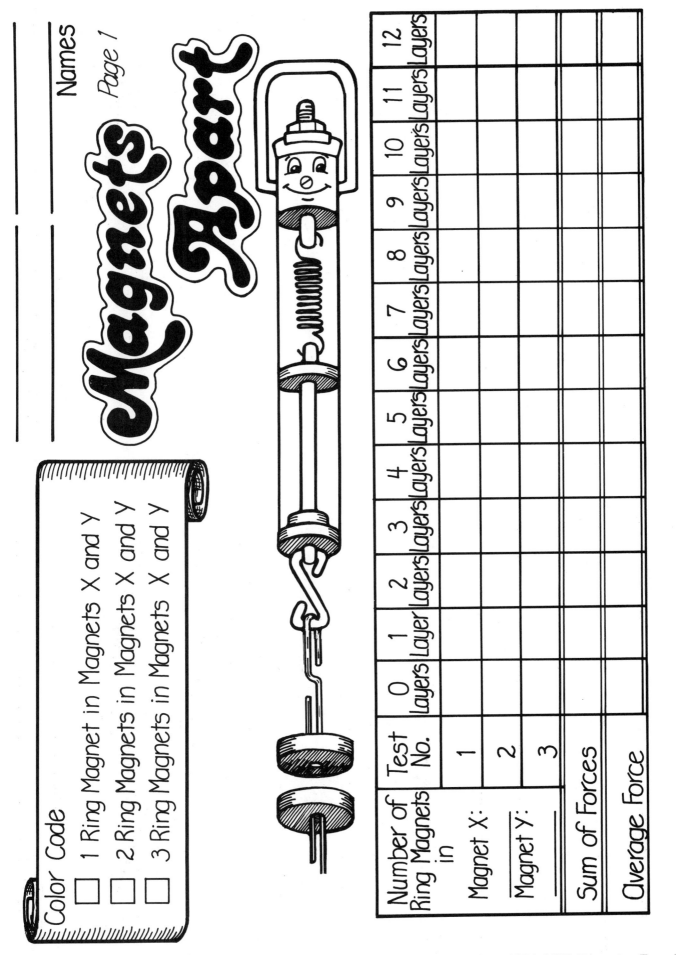

Names _____

Magnets Apart

Page 1

Color Code
- ☐ 1 Ring Magnet in Magnets X and Y
- ☐ 2 Ring Magnets in Magnets X and Y
- ☐ 3 Ring Magnets in Magnets X and Y

Number of Ring Magnets in	Test No.	0 Layers	1 Layer	2 Layers	3 Layers	4 Layers	5 Layers	6 Layers	7 Layers	8 Layers	9 Layers	10 Layers	11 Layers	12 Layers
Magnet X:	1													
	2													
Magnet Y:	3													
Sum of Forces														
Average Force														

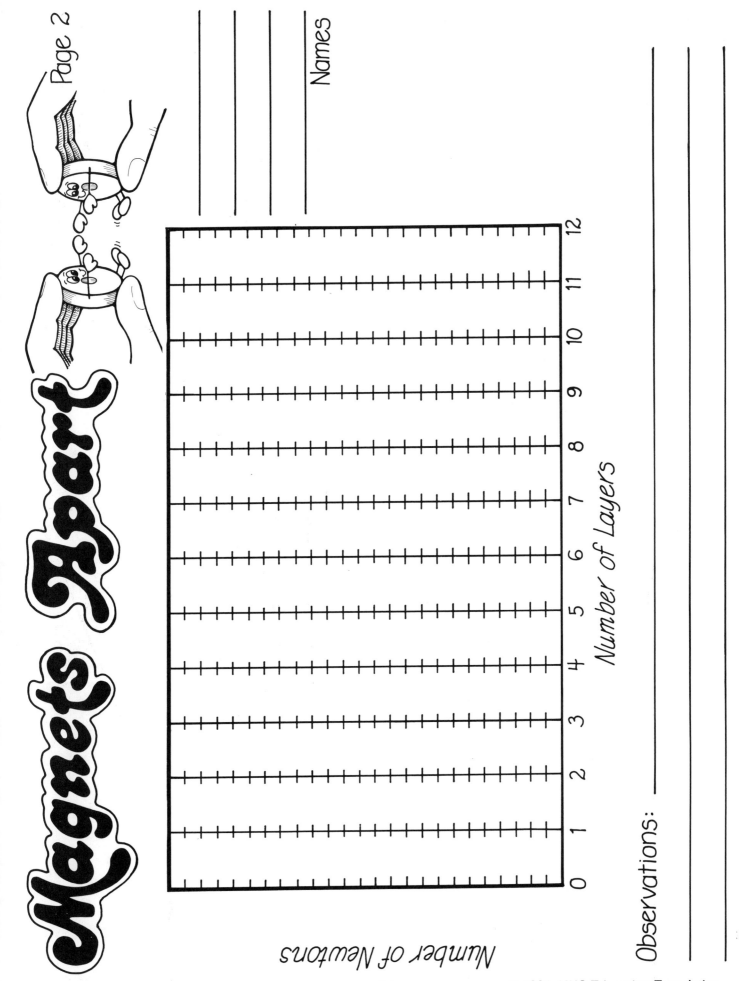

Names

Number of Layers

Number of Newtons

Observations: _____

MOSTLY MAGNETS

© 1991 AIMS Education Foundation

Other Activities Using Magnets

Manual Dexterity

1. Turn a stainless steel bowl (or tuna can made of magnetic materials) upside down.
2. Balance a nail (or needle) on the bowl by holding a magnet above it. Avoid touching the nail with the magnet.

Which Lifts Which?

1. Put a heavy object near a lighter magnet. Which one moves?
2. Put a light object near a heavier magnet. Which one moves?
3. Put an object and a magnet of about the same mass near one another. Which one moves? What pattern do you think you see? Continue to test more objects and magnets to see if you were right. Can you explain what happens?

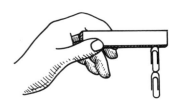

Where is a Magnet Strongest?

1. Hold a bar magnet horizontally.
2. Hang paper clips or staples from various parts of it, as shown. Hang them magnetically, not by hooking them together. The clips gain some magnetism by *induction* or *induced magnetism*.
3. Where can you hang the most clips? Where is a magnet strongest? (near the poles) . . .weakest? (halfway between the poles)

Residual Magnetism

1. Hang paper clips on a magnet, as shown.
2. Remove the longest chain from the magnet. If the clips stay together, it is because of *residual magnetism*.
3. Try not to move. See how long before the clips lose their residual magnetism and fall apart.
4. Are any of the clips magnets now? To find out, hold one to each end of a compass needle. A magnet will attract one end of the needle and repel the other.

Pick Up Clips

1. Slip a toothpick into each of 10-15 paper clips (where paper would go).
2. Drop them onto a table.
3. Using a magnet, try to pick up one at a time without moving any of the others.
4. When used for a game, disturbing another pick means the end of a turn. If desired, dip pick ends into paint or food coloring, and assign point values for the various colors.

Dividing a Magnet

1. Magnetize a large, straightened paper clip by stroking with a magnet.
2. Use two magnetic compasses to identify the poles.
3. Cut the wire. *Immediately* check the *cut* ends. What has happened there?

Turning Off a Compass

1. Position a magnetic compass so that it points north.
2. Challenge students to do something that will *turn if off* so that it does not point north. Supply a variety of magnets plus magnetic and nonmagnetic materials including plastic cups, tuna and taller cans without ends, steel embroidery hoops, etc.

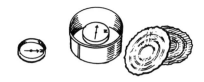

Using the Earth's Magnetic Field

1. Using a magnetic compass for guidance, place a large (demagnetized) rod or bolt so that it points toward magnetic north. Dip the north end downward if you are in the Northern Hemisphere, south end downward in the Southern Hemisphere.
2. With a hammer, tap the higher end 20-30 times. Measure the bolt's magnetism by picking up staples with it.
3. For comparison, place an identical rod in an east-west position; tap it and test similarly.

How Does Heat Affect Magnetism?

1. Stroke a needle to magnetize it. Test it by picking up staples.
2. Hold one end of the needle in the flame of a candle for a few seconds.
3. Now test it again. (If you heated it to the *Curie Point*, the needle was demagnetized.)

3-D Magnetic Fields

1. Using a compass, identify the north end of one magnet and the south end of another.
2. Fill a small jar with cooking oil. Add some iron bits.
3. Cover tightly and shake the jar to distribute iron bits.
4. Immediately hold two magnets on either side of the jar with opposite poles touching the jar.
5. What you observe is the magnetic field around the ends of the magnets. (Keep the jar *as is* for future explorations, perhaps in an interest center.)

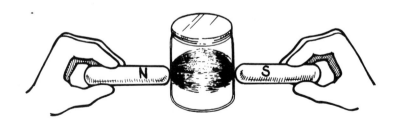

SCIENCE INFORMATION

Magnets are more important in our daily life than most of us realize. They help to change electrical signals into sound in our telephones, radios and television sets. They are essential for radar, microwave ovens, and computers. Magnets are also used extensively to make our electricity.

Historical Background

The word magnet is derived from Magnesia, the name of a region of Greece where certain dark, metallic rocks called *lodestones* were found in ancient times. Lodestone is really a kind of *magnetite*, a hard rock with high iron content and magnetic properties. People in Europe and also in China discovered that if a lodestone were placed on a piece of wood and then floated in a bowl of water, the same part of the lodestone would always point toward the Polestar or North Star. This earliest magnetic *compass*, also called a *directional* or *navigational* compass, was welcomed by mariners, especially for use on long voyages when stars and familiar shore landmarks were not available to guide them.

As with other of the world's major scientific discoveries, many changes have been made to improve the usefulness of the magnetic compass. A magnetized needle replaced the lodestone. By the thirteenth century, the needle was placed on a pivot, so it could move more freely. A number of changes in the compass and its base enabled mariners to read it, even when seas were rough. The discovery of the magnetic north pole and the building of iron ships prompted still other refinements. At first, only the cardinal compass points (north, south, west, east) were identified on compasses. The desire for more precise markings led to the identification of the degrees of a circle. Throughout the history of the compass, the basic principle of the magnetic compass has remained the same. Even in this computer age, it is still numbered among navigational tools considered essential.

Magnetic Poles

The earth acts as if there were a large bar magnet running from north to south through the middle of it. The *magnetic north pole* is not at the earth's geographic north pole; it moves constantly and has even traded places with the south magnetic pole a number of times. At present (1991),

it is located near Bathurst Island, north of mainland Canada and about 1,000 miles from the geographic North Pole. It is moving at the rate of about fifteen miles per year.

Individual magnets also have magnetic poles with unique but consistent characteristics. Magnetic force is always strongest at the poles. Normal magnets have two poles; in industry or research they may have more but usually an even number. There can never be a magnet with only one pole. If two magnets are placed *facing* each other with like magnetic poles together, they will repel one another; if unlike poles are together, they will attract. If a magnet is broken, each piece becomes another complete magnet with the correct, complementary pole forming at each of the broken ends.

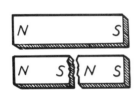

When two (or more) magnets are joined with unlike poles together, they become one combined magnetic force and are considered one magnet. Such a magnet made up of two magnets will be stronger than one magnet but not quite as strong as the combined strength of the two magnets tested separately. If additional magnets are added, the increment will be less each time.

If a magnet pivots or hangs freely on a string, what we call its north pole points as it does because its magnetic field is interacting with that of the earth. Since *opposite* poles attract one another, however, the north pole of one magnet cannot possibly attract the north pole of another. The unavoidable explanation is that one of these poles must really be a south pole. The magnet's south pole must be attracting the earth's north pole, and the magnet's north pole must be attracting the earth's south pole. So which north pole is misnamed and how have scientists tried to solve this paradox? One solution would be to change the identification of one of these north poles to south, to say—for example—that it is the south pole of a magnetic compass that points toward the north magnetic pole; some scientists have adopted this terminology. Another solution, which seems to have been more widely adopted, is to refer to the geographic poles as *north* and *south* (as before), and then to call what is really a magnet's *south* pole its north-*seeking* pole. Similarly, the pole of a magnet that points to the south magnetic pole is called its south-*seeking* pole. Although we frequently shorten these to *north* and *south* poles, it is important for students to understand why the terms *north-seeking* and *south-seeking* are much more accurate than *north* and *south* when referring to magnets.

Magnetic Domains

Why do magnets and magnetic materials act the way they do? The answer lies in the fact that iron and other magnetic materials are made up of very small areas called *magnetic domains.* Each domain consists of billions of atoms. The atoms within each individual domain are always perfectly aligned magnetically. In contrast, the domains themselves may or may not be aligned.

Physicists are constantly learning more about *domain alignment,* and even the definition of the terminology has changed. Until recently it was thought that when domains become aligned, they change the direction in which they point. Current research indicates, however, that in the process of domain alignment, the domains pointing in the right direction probably become larger at the expense of those pointing in other directions.

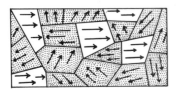
Unaligned

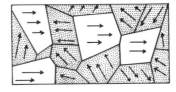
Partially aligned

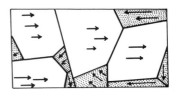
Mostly aligned

The proportion of domains that are aligned determines the amount of magnetic force a magnet has. A piece of pure iron might have almost all unaligned domains and very little magnetic strength. If a moderately strong magnet is held near this iron or strokes it, some of the iron's domains will become aligned and it will exhibit some magnetic properties.

How do the iron's domains know which way to align themselves? The answer depends on the pole of the magnet used to touch or stroke the iron. Since opposites attract, touching or stroking the iron with the south-seeking pole of a magnet will make that end of the iron the north-seeking pole, and the domains facing in a north-seeking direction will be the ones to grow. If only a few domains become aligned, the object will become slightly magnetic; if most of the domains become aligned, the material will be much more strongly magnetic. No material ever has all of its domains aligned.

Magnetic Fields and Field Lines

A *magnetic field* exists in the magnet and in the space around it. Magnetic fields are strongest near the north-seeking and south-seeking poles. The shape of a magnet's magnetic field can be shown by using iron bits or filings to reveal the *magnetic field lines* that spread out in all directions from the north-seeking pole and back in extended arcs to the

south-seeking pole. The magnetic field exists in the whole area: that is, in the spaces between the lines as well as on the lines themselves.

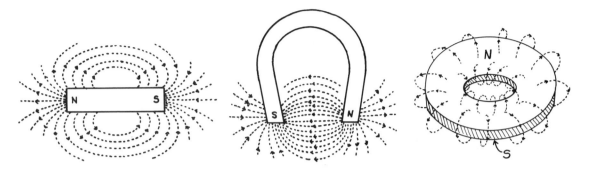

Magnetic fields are able to pass through nonmagnetic materials. This can be demonstrated by placing a piece of paper (a nonmagnetic material) between a magnet and a small magnetic object such as a paper clip; the magnetic interaction through the paper should be readily observable. If, however, the distance between the magnet and the clip is increased, the interaction may become too weak to be observed, even though the magnetic fields are still present. The effect of such nonmagnetic materials on the magnetic interaction is negligible; the main factor is the distance involved.

The effect of the magnetic materials on the situation is different. If the magnet and the clip (or two magnets) are placed on a table on opposite sides of a *tin* (steel) can and outside it, the magnetic fields will go around the can. If, on the other hand, the magnet and the clip are put inside and outside the bottom of the can, there will be magnetic interaction between them through the magnetic material. There will also be some induced magnetism by which the can takes on some magnetism; however, the clip should move when the magnet is moved, showing that the interaction is between the magnet and the clip. If, however, the magnet is too weak, the magnetic object too massive, or the distance between them is too great, the effects of the magnetic interaction may not be observable even though the magnetic fields are still present.

If a magnetic compass is placed on the table with a tin can (both ends removed) over it, the magnetic needle of the compass will stop pointing north. This is called *shielding*. Since the magnetic field lines will always take the easiest pathway, they go around the can rather than through it. If you try this, rotate the can to see if what is happening is really shielding. In fact, the magnetic needle may be attracted to the solder in the can's seam or a part of the can in which the steel is a bit thicker. If this happens, try a seamless can or use several cans of various sizes inside one another.

Here is another application of shielding, one often used in research or manufacturing when the process involves magnetic materials. If the compass in the exploration described above is replaced with a piece of iron

and then two magnets held as shown in the diagram below, the iron would be shielded from the magnetic fields of the magnets.

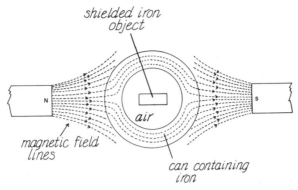

All substances actually display magnetic properties, but most show them to such a very small degree that we usually consider these materials *nonmagnetic*. Highly sophisticated scientific equipment is needed to detect magnetic characteristics at such low levels. On the other hand, a few metallic elements display magnetic properties strongly enough to be considered magnetic, or—more properly—*ferromagnetic* (the *ferro-* means iron). These include iron, nickel, cobalt, rare earths, plus some of their alloys like steel and strontium ferrite. All metals are not considered magnetic, a common misconception easily corrected by observing a common magnet's effect on brass, copper, or aluminum.

Magnetism as an Interaction

Magnetism is usually defined and demonstrated by focussing on an individual magnet and its magnetic field. This promotes a popular misconception that magnetic action centers on each magnet. The reality, quite the opposite, is represented by the term *magnetic interaction*. There must always be an interaction, between magnetic fields, either between two magnets or between a magnet and a material such as soft iron in which a magnetic field can be induced. In other words, a magnet does not ever just lie dormant by itself somewhere; even when no one is using it to attract or repel things, its magnetic field is always busy interacting with other magnetic fields. Although this interaction is often not observable, it is important to know and teach that it is always happening.

The concept of magnetic interaction is based on *Newton's Third Law*, which states that for each action there is an equal and opposite reaction. For example, a revolving lawn sprinkler sprays water in one direction (the action) while the sprinkler turns the other way (the reaction). A less

obvious illustration is that of dropping a stone on the ground. As it hits the ground and bounces slightly, the earth also withdraws imperceptibly. When this same law is applied to magnetism and magnetic activity, it is clear that the force of attraction a magnet experiences toward an object is equal in magnitude to the force the object experiences in being attracted to the magnet.

Attraction and repulsion would seem to be two types of magnetic force, but such is not the case. They are really two manifestations of a single magnetic force. A magnet can only attract (not repel) magnetic materials unless those materials have been magnetized. Two magnets attract or repel each other because their magnetic fields are in a certain orientation, a specific spatial position, with either like or unlike poles together. Although the mathematically measured magnitudes of these two orientations are always equal, factors such as friction or gravity may prevent this equality from being proven precisely in the classroom.

In this book, a conscious effort has been made to use familiar vocabulary. As a result, magnets are referred to in this book as *attracting* or *repelling* materials, and objects are said to *stick to* magnets. These are not contradictions of the magnetic interaction concept, but attempts to help students build on terms most of them already use. Needless to say, it is expected that students will increase their understanding of magnetism and correct their misconceptions about it as they participate in the various investigations. In addition, it is imperative that students learn to use and understand the term magnetic interaction as soon as possible.

It is appropriate to think of magnetism this way:
- Magnetic fields interact with each other.
- A magnet attracts magnetic materials. (It can't repel them.)
- Magnets attract or repel each other.

Magnetism and Electricity

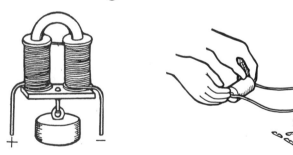

Types of electromagnets

Although scientists still do not feel they completely understand how magnetism works, they have learned much about it through the years. One of the aspects in which much progress has been made is the production of magnetic fields by the movement of electric charges. This

is easy to observe in a *solenoid* or an *electromagnet*. A solenoid is a coil insulated wire connected to a source of electrical power. When an electric current moves through the wire coil, a magnet field is produced. (Remember, current from a battery is electric current.) When a core of soft iron is placed inside the coil, the solenoid becomes an electromagnet. In others words, an electromagnet is a solenoid wound around a piece of pure iron.

But what produces a magnetic field in a permanent magnet where there is no apparent movement of an electric charge? In order to understand this, remember that a magnet, like all objects, is made up of atoms. Each atom consists of a positively charged nucleus surrounded by negatively charged electrons. Even when a magnet lies still, it contains atoms in which the electrons spin and move around the nucleus, somewhat like the way the earth rotates and revolves around the sun. Each spinning electron acts like a small magnet. Each pair of electrons that spin in opposite directions cancel out each others' magnetic fields. In most materials, most magnetism is cancelled out in this way; in each iron atom, however, there are four electrons whose magnetic fields are not canceled. This makes each iron atom a tiny magnet. Some other elements, such as nickel, cobalt, or the rare earths, are magnetic to a lesser degree. In many common magnets, made from alloys containing these elements, the spin described above provides virtually all of the magnetic properties within the domains.

Magnetism was thought to be totally independent of electricity until it was discovered in the early 1800's that an electric current could deflect a compass needle. Since then, scientists have studied both electrical and magnetic phenomena, as well as the relationship between the two. In both, likes repel and opposites attract, poles for magnets, charges for electricity. Both forces can attract or repel without touching. On the other hand, the two opposing types of electrical charges can be separated and then isolated in a way magnetic poles never can, because of the inevitability of having two poles on every magnet.

How Magnets Are Magnetized and Demagnetized

Most ferromagnetic materials do not act like magnets, but they can be magnetized to an observable extent in several ways. Although magnetic strength is relative, depending on the proportion of domains that have been aligned, magnets are often classified in two groups, permanent and temporary.

Permanent magnets are made out of steel (*hard iron*) or certain other magnetic alloys. One method is to stroke the hard iron with a magnet; a pair of steel scissors that has been stroked properly will become magnetized and will retain the magnetism permanently. The magnetic strength of the scissors magnet will be limited by the strength of the magnet that

stroked it. It should be noted that the term permanent is used in a relative sense; as is explained later, permanent magnets can lose some of their strength under certain conditions.

Most *temporary* (or *soft*) *magnets* are made of pure (soft) iron. If a magnet lies near a soft iron object, for example, *induced magnetism* occurs. There is an alignment of domains and the object will display low level magnetic properties for a short time. An electromagnet can also be used to produce temporary magnets. A bar of soft iron is used so that it can be demagnetized and controlled more easily. The magnetism of an electromagnet can be very strong, but it ends every time the current is turned off. Large electromagnets of this type are used in factories and automobile junkyards so that heavy pieces of iron or steel can be picked up and then released whenever the user pushes the right buttons. In solenoids, the button you push moves the iron in and out.

Magnets vary greatly in strength according to a number of factors including what materials they were made from, how they were made, how old they are, and how they have been treated. When they are demagnetized, the aligned domains lose their alignment and shrink. This loss of magnetic strength can take place suddenly or gradually. Electromagnets are demagnetized suddenly each time the power is turned off; permanent or temporary magnets lose some of their magnetism when they are dropped or hammered in a weak magnetic field. It is interesting that in a strong magnetic field (such as when you make a *scissors magnet*), tapping the magnetic object can sometimes help to align the domains and magnetize it, while in a weak magnetic field, tapping or dropping the magnet will weaken it. To keep magnets strong, store them side by side, with unlike poles together, and with what is called a *keeper* (a piece of soft iron) on top of them. Each horseshoe magnet should have its own keeper.

Magnetic Materials in Soil

Soil is made up of mineral particles mixed with varying amounts of humus (animal and vegetable matter). Soil is found in the top layer of the earth's surface. The mineral particles in soil are classified by particle size: sand, silt, and clay. What we commonly refer to as *sand* is really a type of soil made up of large size particles without much humus.

The amount of humus (which is nonmagnetic) in soil will affect the proportion of magnetic material a given soil sample contains. Since sand has less humus, it will have a higher proportion of magnetic particles; for the same reason, soil with more humus is sure to contain magnetic material but in lower proportions. The magnetic particles in soil consist of magnetite (a form of iron) plus some ilmenite and a few micrometeorites. In all of these there is sufficient iron content for them to be attracted by magnets of moderate strength. (See *Mining with Magnets*.)

Sources of Magnets and Other Supplies

In educational activities, several different types and shapes of magnets are used: bar, cow, horseshoe, disc, and ring. Since many bar magnets have limited strength and magnetic life, many teachers are finding ceramic ring magnets a more useful alternative. Because of their strength, low cost, and long magnetic life, they are often recommended for use in AIMS activities. Horseshoe magnets are simply bar magnets bent into that shape, so that the two poles are near one another with a strong magnetic field between them; inexpensive horseshoe magnets sold in variety stores have limited usefulness because of their weakness and short magnetic life. Rolls of magnetic tape are available at craft or fabric stores; these are useful for making refrigerator magnets or other similar projects because of their low cost.

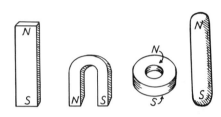

Growing in popularity is the *cow magnet*, a powerful, cylindrical, round-ended shaped magnet. Before these were available, the bits of hay wire and other magnetic scrap would become lodged in the honeycomb-like hexagonal cells of the mucous membrane in the cow's reticulum or second stomach. The motion of the cow would cause some of the wires to perforate the walls of the cow's digestive tract and even its heart. When a cow swallows a cow magnet, the magnet is usually heavy enough to remain in the reticulum, where it attracts most of the magnetic scrap and solves the problem for the rest of the cow's life.

Magnets may be obtained from a number of sources. Natural magnets, found in many parts of the world, are often available at lapidary shops; ask for magnetite, lodestone, or magnetic iron ore. Magnet kits are available directly from AIMS. Magnets may also be available locally from radio/electronic supply stores, farm supply stores, dairy farms, or veterinary supply stores. Since small disc-shaped magnets are a necessary part of loudspeakers, they may often be obtained at low or no cost from discarded speakers at radio repair shops. These magnets are usually about one inch in diameter, a good size and strength for many hands-on activities such as those in this book.

Many magnet activities utilize *iron filings*. Although these may be purchased from scientific supply companies, it is less expensive (and better science education!) to obtain what we call *iron bits* directly from sand or other soil referred to in the previous section and described in detail in *Mining with Magnets*. Somewhat similar filings may be obtained by filing or scraping an iron nail. Rubbing two pieces of steel wool together will produce short pieces of wire. These are satisfactory for some

investigations, but in others they are unsatisfactory because the wires hook onto each other; care should be taken to wash off with *cold* water because the steel wool wires can become lodged in skin.

A Word of Caution

Since magnets are essential to the functioning of some appliances, it is possible to cause damage to them by holding a magnet too close. Magnets can also erase video tapes, audio tapes, and credit cards. Although we do not want to overburden students with negative restrictions that could dampen their enthusiasm, it is important to communicate some sensible safety precautions. *The caution signs provided should be discussed and posted before any lessons on magnetism are taught, so that as students explore with magnets (either at school or at home) they do not cause damage.* Once this is done, encourage everyone to relax and enjoy the wonderful world of magnets.

Glossary

align   to line up or place in correct position; in magnetic materials, refers to the domains becoming aligned or losing alignment resulting in the gain or loss of magnetic force

alnico a combination of aluminum, nickel, and cobalt used to make strong, permanent magnets.

attract   draw or pull, as when two magnets are placed with unlike poles together and their magnetic fields interact

ceramic magnet a magnet that is usually made of strontium ferrite, a form of iron

cow magnet   a cylindrical, round-ended alnico magnet placed in a cow's stomach to prevent injury by loose wire in feed.

demagnetize   make the magnetic field weaker, lesson magnetic strength

domain   in a magnet, a small area made up of billions of atoms; each domain is a tiny magnet with a north and south pole

electromagnet   a temporary magnet made of a piece of iron within a coil of insulated wire; when electric current passes through the wire, the iron becomes a magnet, but when the current is turned off, the iron loses most of its magnetic strength

ferromagnetic   word used to describe an object which can become a magnet; ferro- means iron, but the term ferromagnetic is used in a general sense rather than being limited to materials containing iron

force   any influence that causes an object to move

hard magnetic material   substance containing a metallic element which can be magnetized into permanent magnets and retain magnetism for relatively long periods of time; nickel, cobalt, and rare earths are all hard magnetically, but iron must be made into steel or some other alloy to be hard

induction   process by which an object with magnetic properties produces similar properties in a nearby magnetic object

iron bits   term used in this book to refer to ferromagnetic particles, especially those found in sand or other soil

iron filings small ferromagnetic particles, usually purchased from scientific supply companies

lodestone   magnetite displaying the properties of a magnet

magnetic   having a magnetic field, displaying magnetic properties

magnetic compass an instrument for indicating direction in relation to the north magnetic pole

magnetic field the area around a magnet in which magnetic force exists

magnetic interaction the mutual action or influence of two (or more) magnetic fields upon each other

magnetite a type of hard rock with high iron content and magnetic properties; also called lodestone or loadstone

newton a unit used to measure force; the amount of force which, acting upon one kilogram of matter, will give it an acceleration of one meter per second for every second the force acts

nonmagnetic not magnetic

north-seeking pole the pole of a magnet which will point to the north magnetic pole if the magnet pivots or swings freely

permanent magnets magnets which retain their magnetism for a relatively long period of time after the magnetizing force is removed

polarity having two opposing poles

pole in a magnet, each of the two ends or faces where the magnetic field is strongest

rare earths certain metallic elements which are not actually rare but are difficult to separate from one another

repel push away, as when two magnets are placed with like poles together and their magnetic fields interact

soft iron pure iron

soft magnetic material an element (metallic) which is magnetized or demagnetized with relative ease; iron is soft magnetically unless other materials are added to make it hard

solenoid a coil of insulated wire through which electricity can be passed; becomes an electromagnet when an iron core is placed inside the solenoid

south-seeking pole the pole of a magnet which will point to the north magnetic pole if the magnet pivots or swings freely

temporary magnets magnets (usually made of soft iron) which lose all or most of their magnetic properties after the magnetizing force is removed; electromagnets are temporary magnets

Making and Using My Magnet Book

On the following pages is a primary-level student activity booklet. Individual pages may be used as the class does an investigation related to each concept, or the whole book may be used as a culminating activity.

To construct the booklet, stack pages as they are here, and either staple or punch holes for yarn.

Suggestions

Since it is a small booklet, you may want to have children design the cover and do any coloring before assembling books.

Threading the yarn and tieing a bow is a good activity for eye-hand coordination! Many children can also punch the holes.

Before using the booklet with students, check that the class has done the related investigations.

My Magnet Book

Junior Scientist

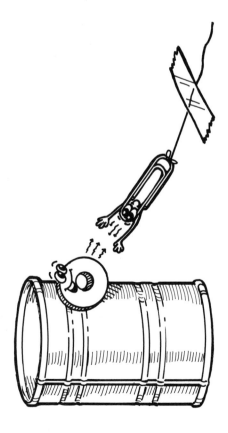

The force of magnetism can *defy* or overcome the force of gravity.

8

A magnet can be made by **stroking** a piece of iron or steel many times with a magnet.

7

Magnets come in many shapes and sizes.

2

108

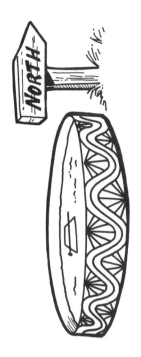

Magnets attract things made of **iron** and other magnetic materials.

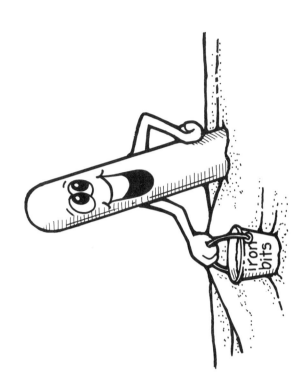

If you float a needle in a dish of water, it will point to the earth's **magnetic north pole.**

Magnets can attract magnetic objects through most materials.

4

Magnets can attract iron bits from sand and other soil.

5

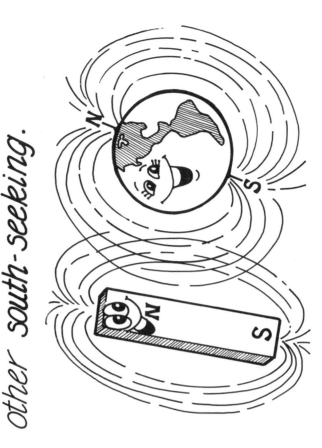

Most magnets have two poles, one north-seeking and the other south-seeking.

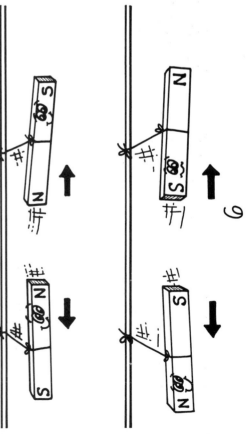

Each magnet has a *magnetic field*. The earth has a magnetic field, too. The magnetic field is strongest at the magnet's *poles*.

3

When two magnets are near one another, they attract or repel. If the north pole of one is near the south pole of the other, they will **attract**.

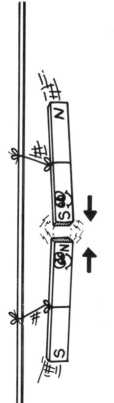

If the north poles or south poles are together, they will repel.

6

Books on Magnets

Here are titles of a few books which may be useful. Although some of them are out of print, they may be available in your school or public library.

Adler, David, *Amazing Magnets*. (Question and Answer Books) Nahwah, NJ: Troll, 1983. (grades 3-6, 32 pages)

Amery, H., A. Littler, Z. Flax, and Pierre Davies, *The Know How Book of Batteries and Magnets*. London: Usborne Pub. Ltd., 1975. (32 pages)

Ardley, Neil, *Exploring Magnetism*. (Action Science Set) New York: Watts, 1984. (grades 4-6, 32 pages)

Brown, Robert J., *333 Science Tricks & Experiments*. Blue Ridge Summit, PA: Tab Books, 1984.

Challand, Helen, *Experiments with Magnets*. (A New True Book) Chicago: Children's Press, 1986

DeBruin, Jerry, *Young Scientists Explore: Electricity and Magnetism*. PO Box 299, Carthage, IL: Good Apple, 1985. (gr. 4-8, 32 pages)

Ferravolo, Rocco V., *Magnets*. Champaign, IL: Garrard, 1960. (64 pages)

Fitzpatrick, Julie, *Magnets*. (Science Spirals Series) Englewood Cliffs, NJ: Silver Burdett, no date available. (gr. 2-5, 32 pages)

Graf, Rudolf F., *Safe and Simple Electrical Electrical Experiments*. New York: Dover, 1973.

Mandell, Muriel, *Simple Science Experiments With Everyday Materials*. Two Park Av, New York, NY 10016: Sterling, 1989.

Marson, Ron, *Magnetism*. 10970 S. Mulino Rd., Canby, OR 97013: TOPS Learning Systems, 1983. (gr. 3-10)

Schmidt, Victor E. and Verne N. Rockcastle, *Teaching Science with Everyday Things*. New York: McGraw-Hill, 1982. (elementary)

Vogt, Gregory, *Electricity and Magnetism*. (First Book Series) New York: Watts, 1985. (gr. 5-8, 84 pages)

Whyman, Kathryn, *Electricity and Magnetism*. (Action Science Series) New York: Gloucester Press, 1986. (32 pages)

The AIMS Program

AIMS is the acronym for "Activities Integrating Mathematics and Science." Such integration enriches learning and makes it meaningful and holistic. AIMS began as a project of Fresno Pacific University to integrate the study of mathematics and science in grades K-9, but has since expanded to include language arts, social studies, and other disciplines.

AIMS is a continuing program of the non-profit AIMS Education Foundation. It had its inception in a National Science Foundation funded program whose purpose was to explore the effectiveness of integrating mathematics and science. The project directors in cooperation with 80 elementary classroom teachers devoted two years to a thorough field-testing of the results and implications of integration.

The approach met with such positive results that the decision was made to launch a program to create instructional materials incorporating this concept. Despite the fact that thoughtful educators have long recommended an integrative approach, very little appropriate material was available in 1981 when the project began. A series of writing projects have ensued and today the AIMS Education Foundation is committed to continue the creation of new integrated activities on a permanent basis.

The AIMS program is funded through the sale of this developing series of books and proceeds from the Foundation's endowment. All net income from program and products flows into a trust fund administered by the AIMS Education Foundation. Use of these funds is restricted to support of research, development, and publication of new materials. Writers donate all their rights to the Foundation to support its on-going program. No royalties are paid to the writers.

The rationale for integration lies in the fact that science, mathematics, language arts, social studies, etc., are integrally interwoven in the real world from which it follows that they should be similarly treated in the classroom where we are preparing students to live in that world. Teachers who use the AIMS program give enthusiastic endorsement to the effectiveness of this approach.

Science encompasses the art of questioning, investigating, hypothesizing, discovering, and communicating. Mathematics is the language that provides clarity, objectivity, and understanding. The language arts provide us powerful tools of communication. Many of the major contemporary societal issues stem from advancements in science and must be studied in the context of the social sciences. Therefore, it is timely that all of us take seriously a more holistic mode of educating our students. This goal motivates all who are associated with the AIMS Program. We invite you to join us in this effort.

Meaningful integration of knowledge is a major recommendation coming from the nation's professional science and mathematics associations. The American Association for the Advancement of Science in *Science for All Americans* strongly recommends the integration of mathematics, science, and technology. The National Council of Teachers of Mathematics places strong emphasis on applications of mathematics such as are found in science investigations. AIMS is fully aligned with these recommendations.

Extensive field testing of AIMS investigations confirms these beneficial results.

1. Mathematics becomes more meaningful, hence more useful, when it is applied to situations that interest students.
2. The extent to which science is studied and understood is increased, with a significant economy of time, when mathematics and science are integrated.
3. There is improved quality of learning and retention, supporting the thesis that learning which is meaningful and relevant is more effective.
4. Motivation and involvement are increased dramatically as students investigate real-world situations and participate actively in the process.

We invite you to become part of this classroom teacher movement by using an integrated approach to learning and sharing any suggestions you may have. The AIMS Program welcomes you!

AIMS Education Foundation Programs

A Day with AIMS

Intensive one-day workshops are offered to introduce educators to the philosophy and rationale of AIMS. Participants will discuss the methodology of AIMS and the strategies by which AIMS principles may be incorporated into curriculum. Each participant will take part in a variety of hands-on AIMS investigations to gain an understanding of such aspects as the scientific/mathematical content, classroom management, and connections with other curricular areas. *A Day with AIMS* workshops may be offered anywhere in the United States. Necessary supplies and take-home materials are usually included in the enrollment fee.

A Week with AIMS

Throughout the nation, AIMS offers many one-week workshops each year, usually in the summer. Each workshop lasts five days and includes at least 30 hours of AIMS hands-on instruction. Participants are grouped according to the grade level(s) in which they are interested. Instructors are members of the AIMS Instructional Leadership Network. Supplies for the activities and a generous supply of take-home materials are included in the enrollment fee. Sites are selected on the basis of applications submitted by educational organizations. If chosen to host a workshop, the host agency agrees to provide specified facilities and cooperate in the promotion of the workshop. The AIMS Education Foundation supplies workshop materials as well as the travel, housing, and meals for instructors.

AIMS One-Week Perspectives Workshops

Each summer, Fresno Pacific University offers AIMS one-week workshops on its campus in Fresno, California. AIMS Program Directors and highly qualified members of the AIMS National Leadership Network serve as instructors.

The Science Festival and the Festival of Mathematics

Each summer, Fresno Pacific University offers a Science Festival and a Festival of Mathematics. These festivals have gained national recognition as inspiring and challenging experiences, giving unique opportunities to experience hands-on mathematics and science in topical and grade-level groups. Guest faculty includes some of the nation's most highly regarded mathematics and science educators. Supplies and take-home materials are included in the enrollment fee.

The AIMS Instructional Leadership Program

This is an AIMS staff-development program seeking to prepare facilitators for leadership roles in science/math education in their home districts or regions. Upon successful completion of the program, trained facilitators may become members of the AIMS Instructional Leadership Network, qualified to conduct AIMS workshops, teach AIMS in-service courses for college credit, and serve as AIMS consultants. Intensive training is provided in mathematics, science, process and thinking skills, workshop management, and other relevant topics.

College Credit and Grants

Those who participate in workshops may often qualify for college credit. If the workshop takes place on the campus of Fresno Pacific University, that institution may grant appropriate credit. If the workshop takes place off-campus, arrangements can sometimes be made for credit to be granted by another college or university. In addition, the applicant's home school district is often willing to grant in-service or professional development credit. Many educators who participate in AIMS workshops are recipients of various types of educational grants, either local or national. Nationally known foundations and funding agencies have long recognized the value of AIMS mathematics and science workshops to educators. The AIMS Education Foundation encourages educators interested in attending or hosting workshops to explore the possibilities suggested above. Although the Foundation strongly supports such interest, it reminds applicants that they have the primary responsibility for fulfilling *current* requirements.

For current information regarding the programs described above, please complete the following:

We invite you to subscribe to $\mathcal{AIMS}$!

Each issue of $\mathcal{AIMS}$ contains a variety of material useful to educators at all grade levels. Feature articles of lasting value deal with topics such as mathematical or science concepts, curriculum, assessment, the teaching of process skills, and historical background. Several of the latest AIMS math/science investigations are always included, along with their reproducible activity sheets. As needs direct and space allows, various issues contain news of current developments, such as workshop schedules, activities of the AIMS Instructional Leadership Network, and announcements of upcoming publications.

$\mathcal{AIMS}$ is published monthly, August through May. Subscriptions are on an annual basis only. A subscription entered at any time will begin with the next issue, but will also include the previous issues of that volume. Readers have preferred this arrangement because articles and activities within an annual volume are often interrelated.

Please note that an $\mathcal{AIMS}$ subscription automatically includes duplication rights for one school site for all issues included in the subscription. Many schools build cost-effective library resources with their subscriptions.

YES! I am interested in subscribing to $\mathcal{AIMS}$.

Name _____   Home Phone _____

Address _____   City, State, Zip _____

Please send the following volumes (subject to availability):

_____ Volume V	(1990-91)	$30.00	_____ Volume X	(1995-96)	$30.00
_____ Volume VI	(1991-92)	$30.00	_____ Volume XI	(1996-97)	$30.00
_____ Volume VII	(1992-93)	$30.00	_____ Volume XII	(1997-98)	$30.00
_____ Volume IX	(1994-95)	$30.00	_____ Volume XIII	(1998-99)	$30.00

_____ **Limited offer: Volumes XIII & XIV (1998-2000) $55.00**

(Note: Prices may change without notice)

Check your method of payment:

❒ Check enclosed in the amount of $ _____

❒ Purchase order attached (Please include the P.O.#, the authorizing signature, and position of the authorizing person.)

❒ Credit Card   ❒ Visa   ❒ MasterCard   Amount $ _____

Card # _____   Expiration Date _____

Signature _____   Today's Date _____

Make checks payable to **AIMS Education Foundation**.
Mail to $\mathcal{AIMS}$ magazine, P.O. Box 8120, Fresno, CA 93747-8120.
Phone (209) 255-4094 or (888) 733-2467 FAX (209) 255-6396
AIMS Homepage: http://www.AIMSedu.org/

AIMS Program Publications

GRADES K-4 SERIES

Bats Incredible
Brinca de Alegria Hacia la Primavera con las Matemáticas y Ciencias
Cáete de Gusto Hacia el Otoño con la Matemática y Ciencias
Cycles of Knowing and Growing
Fall Into Math and Science
Field Detectives
Glide Into Winter With Math and Science
Hardhatting in a Geo-World (Revised Edition, 1996)
Jaw Breakers and Heart Thumpers (Revised Edition, 1995)
Los Cincos Sentidos
Overhead and Underfoot (Revised Edition, 1994)
Patine al Invierno con Matemáticas y Ciencias
Popping With Power (Revised Edition, 1996)
Primariamente Física (Revised Edition, 1994)
Primarily Earth
Primariamente Plantas
Primarily Physics (Revised Edition, 1994)
Primarily Plants
Sense-able Science
Spring Into Math and Science
Under Construction

GRADES K-6 SERIES

Budding Botanist
Critters
El Botanista Principiante
Mostly Magnets
Ositos Nada Más
Primarily Bears
Principalmente Imanes
Water Precious Water

GRADES 5-9 SERIES

Actions with Fractions
Brick Layers
Conexiones Eléctricas
Down to Earth
Electrical Connections
Finding Your Bearings (Revised Edition, 1996)
Floaters and Sinkers (Revised Edition, 1995)
From Head to Toe
Fun With Foods
Gravity Rules!
Historical Connections in Mathematics, Volume I
Historical Connections in Mathematics, Volume II
Historical Connections in Mathematics, Volume III
Machine Shop
Magnificent Microworld Adventures
Math + Science, A Solution
Off the Wall Science: A Poster Series Revisited
Our Wonderful World
Out of This World (Revised Edition, 1994)
Pieces and Patterns, A Patchwork in Math and Science
Piezas y Diseños, un Mosaic de Matemáticas y Ciencias
Soap Films and Bubbles
Spatial Visualization
The Sky's the Limit (Revised Edition, 1994)
The Amazing Circle, Volume 1
Through the Eyes of the Explorers:
    Minds-on Math & Mapping
What's Next, Volume 1
What's Next, Volume 2
What's Next, Volume 3

For further information write to:
AIMS Education Foundation • P.O. Box 8120 • Fresno, California 93747-8120

AIMS Duplication Rights Program

AIMS has received many requests from school districts for the purchase of unlimited duplication rights to AIMS materials. In response, the AIMS Education Foundation has formulated the program outlined below. There is a built-in flexibility which, we trust, will provide for those who use AIMS materials extensively to purchase such rights for either individual activities or entire books.

It is the goal of the AIMS Education Foundation to make its materials and programs available at reasonable cost. All income from the sale of publications and duplication rights is used to support AIMS programs; hence, strict adherence to regulations governing duplication is essential. Duplication of AIMS materials beyond limits set by copyright laws and those specified below is strictly forbidden.

Limited Duplication Rights

Any purchaser of an AIMS book may make up to *200 copies* of any activity in that book for use at *one school site*. Beyond that, rights must be purchased according to the appropriate category.

Unlimited Duplication Rights for Single Activities

An individual or school may purchase the right to make an unlimited number of copies of a single activity. The royalty is $5.00 per activity per school site.

Examples: 3 activities x 1 site x $5.00 = $15.00
9 activities x 3 sites x $5.00 = $135.00

Unlimited Duplication Rights for Entire Books

A school or district may purchase the right to make an unlimited number of copies of a single, *specified* book. The royalty is $20.00 per book per school site. This is in addition to the cost of the book.

Examples: 5 books x 1 site   x $20.00 = $100.00
12 books x 10 sites x $20.00 = $2400.00

Magazine/Newsletter Duplication Rights

Those who purchase *AIMS* (magazine)/*Newsletter* are hereby granted permission to make up to 200 copies of any portion of it, provided these copies will be used for educational purposes.

Workshop Instructors' Duplication Rights

Workshop instructors may distribute to registered workshop participants a maximum of 100 copies of any article and/or 100 copies of no more than eight activities, provided these six conditions are met:

1. Since all AIMS activities are based upon the *AIMS Model of Mathematics* and the *AIMS Model of Learning*, leaders must include in their presentations an explanation of these two models.
2. Workshop instructors must relate the AIMS activities presented to these basic explanations of the AIMS philosophy of education.
3. The copyright notice must appear on all materials distributed.
4. Instructors must provide information enabling participants to order books and magazines from the Foundation.
5. Instructors must inform participants of their limited duplication rights as outlined below.
6. Only student pages may be duplicated.

Written permission must be obtained for duplication beyond the limits listed above. Additional royalty payments may be required.

Workshop Participants' Rights

Those enrolled in workshops in which AIMS student activity sheets are distributed may duplicate a maximum of 35 copies or enough to use the lessons one time with one class, whichever is less. Beyond that, rights must be purchased according to the appropriate category.

Application for Duplication Rights

The purchasing agency or individual must clearly specify the following:
1. Name, address, and telephone number
2. Titles of the books for Unlimited Duplication Rights contracts
3. Titles of activities for Unlimited Duplication Rights contracts
4. Names and addresses of school sites for which duplication rights are being purchased.

NOTE: Books to be duplicated must be purchased separately and are not included in the contract for Unlimited Duplication Rights.

The requested duplication rights are automatically authorized when proper payment is received, although a *Certificate of Duplication Rights* will be issued when the application is processed.

Address all correspondence to: **Contract Division**
AIMS Education Foundation
P.O. Box 8120
Fresno, CA 93747-8120